Th

Corporate

BIRBAL

VIVEK VAIDYA

FINGERPRINT!

Published by

FiNGERPRINT!
An imprint of Prakash Books India Pvt. Ltd

113/A, Darya Ganj,
New Delhi-110 002
Email: info@prakashbooks.com/sales@prakashbooks.com

 Fingerprint Publishing
 @FingerprintP
 @fingerprintpublishingbooks
www.fingerprintpublishing.com

ISBN: 978 93 6214 362 4

Dedicated to all my colleagues who said they benefitted from my Birbal stories in difficult situations at work.

Acknowledgment

The concept of *The Corporate Birbal* was probably born when I got the opportunity to lead a team. My team members would come to me for advice, and I would tell them, "Being right is not enough, you should be seen as being right." Often, they found this concept difficult to understand or implement. That is when I would tell them a Birbal story, which would prove my point.

Birbal, as the legend describes, was a Hindu minister working for a Muslim emperor, therefore, constantly under scrutiny from peers. The emperor was kind but would test him all the time to keep him on the edge. It is sufficient to say that he operated in the most politically volatile environment one can imagine. Yet, he emerged victorious by being politically correct. This quality of Birbal attracted me.

At work, we all work in a politically charged environment. Most of us are focused on performance and skills, which are directly under our control. However, we often lack the political wisdom that came so naturally to Birbal. That is why I thought of bringing Birbal out of childhood storybooks and putting him back on the map in the corporate world where he is needed the most.

The protagonist in my novel, Sid, is a bright, intelligent, smart and hardworking entrepreneur with fire in the belly. The only thing he lacks is wisdom. Neither is it taught in his business school, nor does he have anyone who could impart it at work. Usually, it is earned with experience over a prolonged period of time, but Sid doesn't have that luxury. He is faced with difficult choices one after another, with no one to guide him. That is when he accidentally discovers Birbal, and through age-old wisdom, Birbal guides him all the way.

I want to acknowledge and thank all my colleagues who have patiently listened to my stories and reassured me that they benefitted from them. The seed of this novel germinated somewhere in those interactions. I want to acknowledge all my employers and bosses who enabled and encouraged me to travel and get varied experiences. Sid is a completely fictional character, but my life experiences helped me to imagine the situations he might encounter and allowed me to describe them realistically. I want to acknowledge my wife, Nalini, who read all my drafts, and offered invaluable suggestions that made the plot, situations and characters interesting. I also want to acknowledge all my friends who volunteered to read the novel and offer constructive feedback.

The Corporate Birbal has been a long journey. I have avoided the temptation of basing the characters on myself, my friends, or colleagues. I have followed the harder way of creating a fictional character, thinking through the personality traits, their motivation, and their behavior. But the good part of this approach is that once the characters were defined, they almost became real people for me. Then the stories, situations, and their dialogues just wrote themselves.

I acknowledge Suhail Mathur from Book Bakers for trusting my offbeat script and putting his energies behind it. And my publisher Fingerprint for taking this up and making it into a beautifully crafted book.

Finally, I acknowledge you, the reader, who has chosen to read this book instead of being glued to the screen. Without your support, this novel won't exist.

CONTENTS

CHAPTER 1

In the Firing Line!

Following in Steve Jobs' footsteps

February 2016

In his plush cabin overlooking the Cubbon Park in Bengaluru, Sid leans back in his chair, looks at his MacBook in disbelief, and starts rubbing his temples. His worst nightmare has come true. Everything that could have gone wrong, has gone wrong. He cannot believe he has to see this shocking email as the CEO of the company he started, nurtured, and brought to this level with sweat and tears. He thinks it is even more ironic that he can't do anything about it. It is impossible to fathom the depth of his despair as he sinks into his seat.

There is a familiar knock on the door. It is Thambi, the coffee guy, a regular, silent visitor to his office for the last seven years. He serves the coffee in two steel cups. The aroma of filter coffee wafts through the cabin. Usually, the first sip of coffee energizes Sid, but today is a different day. Even his favorite coffee fails to alter his mood.

Sid's cabin is very modern. It is all-glass, equipped with motorized blinders, and most of its fixtures are controlled via an application on Sid's iPad. Sid can make the cabin into a private room, control the light, air conditioning, and other amenities with a flick of a button on his App. His work table is in a corner diagonally opposite the entrance. On the right, there is a small roundtable surrounded by five chairs. On a table in a heap, there are writing pads, sharpened wooden pencils, colorful post-it pads, and colored markers. It is a brainstorming area.

Sid's instructions to the interior designers of his cabin were to keep one side of the whole cabin free from any electronic gadgets and screens. He believes any kind of screen makes you efficient but not creative. The brainstorming area has witnessed many out-of-the-box, unconventional ideas that have helped Sid impress clients—the very same ideas that propelled the company to dizzying heights in a very short period.

The area on the left has two plush sofa beds with a large flat-screen TV. Sid himself has spent countless nights sleeping on the sofa beds. There is a small showcase that has multiple mementos, certificates, and gifts that Sid has received from customers in various conferences and award ceremonies. There are also a few potted plants in a corner to provide a little more of a natural look to the plush cabin.

In a way, the steel cups do not really 'fit in' with the look, but Sid doesn't care. He insists filter coffee doesn't taste the same unless it is steaming out of the metal containers. Pensively, he takes a sip and reads the email once again.

Dear Sid,

For the last decade, our company Creativity Unlimited has grown from a start-up to a unicorn. We have graduated from a one-bedroom apartment to 20,000 square feet posh offices, and our revenues and profits have grown multifold. All this would not have been possible without your wholehearted contribution and support. You have worked very hard for the company for the last decade to bring it to this level. We are thankful for your contribution so far.

However, at this juncture, the company needs a fresh direction, a new start, and a different strategy. Over the past few months, we had a lot of discussions with you, and it is quite clear that despite best efforts, significant differences remain between the Board of Directors on one side and you as CEO on the other. The Board, therefore, thinks that it is best to look for fresh leadership which is better aligned with our direction.

We really value you as a co-founder of this company; hence, your stake in the company remains intact and you may be able to encash it at a suitable time in the future.

We do hope that you take this in the right spirit.

Feel free to let us know when you would like to move out.

Sincerely yours,

Paul

On behalf of the Board of Directors of Creativity Unlimited

Sid looks up. Creativity Unlimited is not just a job for Sid, it has been his life for the past decade. His disbelief at being fired from the company he started is palpable, hanging in the air like smoke from a cigarette. He doesn't even have anyone to talk to about this. Friendships, relationships—where was the time? Ever since he completed his Post-Graduate Diploma in Business Management from the Indian Institute of Management, Bengaluru, all that he has done is work. He invested so much time in this company that there was no time to nurture any friendships. The nature of a workaholic is a lonely one. The only person he can think of is Anjali. He takes his phone out, looks at her number, but doesn't dare to dial.

I haven't spoken to her for the last three years. I had the audacity to call off the trip she had planned so meticulously. I didn't even apologize properly. I have no right to call her, not this time, Sid thinks to himself and puts his phone back on the table.

Continuing his introspection while sipping his coffee, Sid looks out of his cabin's window, taking in the entire office. The office isn't your run-of-the-mill boring professional workspace. There are no cubicles, desks, or chairs. Instead, bean bags, pillows, and sofas are strewn around the office floor. There are no designated workspaces for anyone. The employees, also called 'buddies', sit wherever they like, and personalize whichever workspace however they want to. The walls are not gray nor blue, but pink, orange, burgundy, and turquoise. There is no dress code, so jeans, shorts, miniskirts, and spaghetti tops are commonplace. Some buddies have exotic potted plants around their work areas, some have expressed themselves with graffiti on the walls, and others display unique showpieces.

What appeared to others as radical ideas were simply products of the adversities Sid faced when he started Creativity Unlimited. He had begun this company in a completely unfurnished one-bedroom flat. Instead of spending money on furniture, he asked his initial employees to bring whatever furniture they liked or could spare. Some brought sofas, some bean bags, and others brought sofa beds. Sid had no money to get the flat painted professionally, so instead, he requested his employees to paint their work sections in whatever color they wanted. Some painted theirs orange, some pink, and some turquoise.

These ideas were instant hits among the newcomers to the company, who saw these things as personalization. They felt an instant connection with the company and its culture. It was precisely this quality that won Creativity Unlimited the 'most sought-after Indian company of the year' award for three consecutive years.

Back then, Sid had decided that if the company wanted to target young customers, they needed young employees who could put themselves in the customers' shoes. He refused to treat his employees like 40-somethings or try to control or monitor them. He wanted them to feel at home, to feel motivated, and they should have fun and express themselves. In fact, he was the one who established the term 'buddies' in place of employees.

When a new buddy joins, they each have an option to choose their nicknames. Sid was of the opinion that, "Our name defines our identity but ironically, this is not something we choose—it is given to us without our consent. It is not something we can change quickly or on a whim either. So, at Creativity Unlimited, every buddy is allowed to choose their nicknames." So, Siddhartha became Sid, Jyotichandrika became Jo and Jeetendraprasad became Jee. For most buddies, this nickname became their identity for the rest of their lives.

Buddies have no fixed office timings, nor do they have to clock in a certain number of hours. They have unlimited leaves, with the only condition to post photographs on the internal website showcasing their escapades. Everything Sid does is unconventional, unheard of, and very risky. But it has paid off. The company is the most sought-after employer, and within two to three years, it has hundreds of applicants with the lowest turnover rates. Sid is very proud of all these achievements. But is likely to become history very soon.

"From a humble beginning in a one-bedroom apartment, we have come a long way," he muses.

Creativity Unlimited is a digital communication agency that operates in a niche field of digital strategies and advertising. When it was founded ten years ago in the age of conventional advertising media that consisted of TV, print, and billboards, not many corporations even knew about the new media that the company worked with, such as YouTube. Sid had spotted this trend too early, back when people claimed the 'Internet was a fad'. This is why Creativity Unlimited is today's most sought-after digital advertising agency.

His mind wanders to the series of events where it all began.

The savior for centuries: Birbal.

March 2006

Sid and his friends are waiting impatiently outside the boardroom of Zen Advertising to present the final project report. All of them are in office attire—a full-sleeved formal shirt, trousers, and a necktie. Most, if not all of them, are not used to wearing a necktie. None of them know if their knots are right. Every few minutes, one of them fiddles with the knot, and another murmurs an unconvincing but reassuring comment on how it looks.

Their project is on new-age digital advertisements. Sid is by far the most passionate contributor to the project, and their project findings are rather disturbing for Zen Advertising. Using Sid's passion for the subject and his level of interest, the project-mates have unanimously nominated him to bell the cat. In other words, Sid will be the bearer of bad news during the presentation.

Understandably, Sid is the fidgetiest one of them all. He stands straight, ignoring his wonky necktie, and stares nervously at the door while the others flip through magazines and look at the pinup boards. Sid knows that he has done his best on this project—his hypothesis carries a warning for companies like Zen, and home-grown advertising agencies, who are refusing to see how the world of advertisements is changing rapidly across the globe.

His report is titled 'Digital Advertisements: A Death Knell for Newspaper and TV Ads.' The title is bold, provocative, and frankly a little scary. All deliberate effects. Sid Uses an aggressive approach, playing on fear to get attention. However, thinking of a clever title and putting together some PowerPoint slides is one thing, and standing in a room full of industry stalwarts, looking into their eyes, and informing them they are wrong, is a whole other ball game.

Then, the moment of truth arrives.

The teammates enter the room and sit in their designated positions. Sid stands up, clears his throat, and begins. "The Indian advertising industry today is worth thousands of crores. There are estimated to be five lakh brands in the Indian market. Forty percent of these brands target customers below the age of thirty, so we have to dive into the media habits of these customers."

He pauses and looks around. About ten grim faces are staring at him, without a hint of friendliness.

Sid continues nervously, "We spoke to these customers in an informal setting, and this is what we found: 58% of the customers could not recall any billboard campaign. They mentioned that they listen to music when they are traveling, 28% of them said that they don't know which newspaper is bought by their household. A whopping 77% could not recall any popular serial on any leading channel. They mentioned that they hate popular TV serials and anything associated with them."

Sid takes a pause and then continues, "For us, these findings are shocking but not unexpected. After we completed this study with unknown respondents, we asked our friends what their media habits were, and the results were similar. So we reckon that something big is about to happen in the Indian advertising industry. Digital media is primed to take over, especially for the younger generation. Conventional advertisements in traditional media such as TV, newspapers, billboards, and in other forms outdoors, are going to die."

There. He said the worst of what he had to say and delivered the news he was dreading. Most of the ten stern faces are now frowning and leaning back in their chairs. Some of them have their hands folded behind their heads. He spots some disapproving heads shaking and some disengagement where people have turned to their laptops instead. Fact-checking him perhaps? Withdrawing them from the uncomfortable news he has just delivered to check their email instead? He doesn't know. The air hangs heavy with extreme hostility. He must do something to turn the tide back in his favor.

"We have a recommendation. Zen Advertising is in a great position to start a digital marketing division that focuses solely on emerging media. We know that this is bound to grow exponentially and one day will overtake conventional media in terms of customer reach and attention."

"Won't this kill our current business, which is extremely profitable and well-established?" One of the executives asks rather curtly. Sid anticipated this question, so he is ready with an answer.

"If you don't disrupt your own business, someone else will. This trend is not something that is going to diminish. Our analysis indicates that this will only grow."

"So you suggest we kill the goose that's laying golden eggs for our company?" Irritation and anger bubbling underneath the surface result in this rhetorical question.

The tension in the room makes Sid loosen his tie-knot.

"What did you say your sample size was? Was the research method scientific?" An executive who was paying close attention asks.

"We don't believe in traditional research methodology. When asked a direct question, a customer usually gives a response that he thinks we want to hear. Insights collected indirectly usually are more accurate."

"So . . . not a scientific method but a more informal one, right?"

"Yes. Correct."

"You are using unscientific research methods and minuscule sample sizes to declare that our business will cease to exist in a few years? The audacity!" . . .

"But sir . . . " Sid doesn't get a chance to complete his sentence—the executive slams his diary shut, angrily smashes his pen back into his pocket, and storms out of the room, muttering under his breath about 'wasting his time' and 'the immaturity of the younger generation'.

Not long after, the other executives follow suit, until only a handful are left in the room.

They offer the group some empty reassurances, "Guys, your study is fascinating, and there are some interesting observations. But as mentioned, this is too small a study for us to comprehensively conclude if this digital trend will really catch up and threaten our existing business. You made a bold prediction by calling that a death knell, but we don't believe this will happen. Unfortunately, we will no longer be interested in pursuing your project, nor would we be interested in discussing this matter with you any further."

Their words are polite but harsh, effectively making it clear that they were requesting Sid and his friends to leave their office. Sid is heartbroken. He can't face his friends as they all trudge out of the conference room. His friends, on the other hand, are outraged. They warned Sid against such adventurism. They didn't necessarily disagree with him but certainly didn't want to stand in front of everyone and tell them that "your business is going to die". They think all their efforts have been wasted, and all because Sid insisted on presenting unpleasant conclusions to industry stalwarts.

They all rush to the lift in their embarrassment. As Sid is entering, they remember that they haven't got the gate pass signed. They tell Sid to get it signed because none of them want to face the executives. Sid turns back with a heavy heart. As the lift descends, he can hear his friends complaining. Sid gets the gate pass signed and comes back into the elevator. Lost in his thoughts, he doesn't notice the other person standing in the lift.

"Your presentation was excellent."

"Oh, sorry. Did you say something to me?"

"Yes! I heard your presentation in the conference room just now. I think you are on the right track."

Sid is half surprised and half curious. "Sorry, there were so many people in the conference room I didn't realize you were there too."

"It's alright. I am not a prominent person in this company. But you should develop this idea more."

"Really? You saw the response we got though—everyone pretty much walked out on us."

"That's more to do with HOW you said what you said, not really because of the content. If you can deliver the message strategically, things could be very different."

"Really?"

"Yes. I really think you are onto something."

"That is very nice of you."

"Have you heard of Akbar-Birbal stories?"

"Err, hmm. Yes, why?"

"Read the story 'Birbal and the Talking Parrot', and you will know how to deliver your message strategically."

The elevator reaches the ground floor. Before Sid can even ask for his name, the person leaves. Sid's friends are waiting for him downstairs, with grim faces ready to berate him for his drastic ideas. But Sid hears nothing—he rides on the elation he feels because of the kind comments of the stranger in the lift.

I should have at least asked for his name, if not a business card. I should have asked what he meant by delivering the message strategically, Sid thinks.

***

On Saturday evenings, Sid and Anjali usually go for dinner dates. Unable to shake the story suggested by the stranger from his mind, Sid decides to buy the book *Stories of Akbar and Birbal* from the nearby bookstore. Instead of meeting at their usual restaurant for dinner, Sid asks Anjali to come to the bookstore.

Anjali is bewildered. "Sid, you know how eagerly I was looking forward to our dinner date this Saturday. I want to tell you everything about my campus interviews. You know, I am this close to getting a job!"

"Of course, I understand, baby! But you know the work for this project is really important to me too, right?"

"Oh, come on, Sid. This is no project work. You're going to buy a children's book, and you can do that anytime."

"So join me, no? You love shopping anyway," Sid says.

"You are not asking me to go to Commercial Street. You are asking me to go to Majestic. It takes too long to get there. If we go there, there is no time left for our date. And going to that boring place together can hardly be called a date."

"I have to go. This is important for me."

"More important than our once-a-week dinner date, Sid?"

There is a long pause.

Sid goes to the Sapna bookstore in Majestic by himself. He finds the book he is looking for—the thickest Akbar and Birbal book in the entire bookstore—and heads back to the hostel.

As soon as he reaches his room, he flips to the Parrot story.

Birbal and the Talking Parrot

Akbar was a noble Mughal king who ruled India in the twelfth century. It is said that he had a very intelligent, witty, and smart advisor called Birbal in his court. Once a traveler from a distant land who had a talking parrot visited Akbar's court. The parrot charmed Akbar and he fell in love with the parrot. He appointed skilled caretakers for the parrot. To ensure that they were serious about the job and understood the importance of the parrot, he warned them, "Whoever tells me the parrot is dead, will get his head chopped off."

It worked like magic and all the caretakers worked round the clock to take care of the parrot.

But they could not avoid the inevitable.

One day the parrot died and the caretakers did not have anyone else but Birbal to go to. As always, Birbal had a trick up his sleeve to bypass the conundrum, which he shared with them.

When Akbar asked about the parrot next time, the caretakers said, "He has been behaving quite strangely. He neither eats nor drinks anything. He has his eyes closed and does not move much."

Surprised, Akbar walked up to the cage and exclaimed, "Oh! The parrot is dead. Why didn't you just say so!"

Birbal said, "It was as per your wishes, sir, everyone knew the parrot was dead but nobody wants their head to be chopped off for delivering this news to you."

Sid reads the story closely for the third time and finally relates it to his own situation.

If Birbal was in front of him, what would he say?

He might say, "Yes, conventional advertisements are in big trouble. Maybe they will indeed be replaced by digital advertisements one day. But for now, this is a 'favorite talking parrot' of many companies around the world. They don't want to hear that the parrot is dead, any more than they want the prediction that the parrot will eventually die. So the key here would be YOU allowing your 'Jahanpanah', who in this case is your client, to conclude the status of the parrot instead."

Understanding this brings a smile to Sid's face. He should describe the new digital medium as a medium that co-exists with conventional advertising rather than declaring death upon traditional advertising mediums.

A sudden realization also dawns on him. Instead of pitching for a digital advertising job to the advertisement companies, he could start his own company to provide that alternative.

Where all of his classmates, including his girlfriend Anjali, are chasing after blue chip companies for a job, the idea of becoming an entrepreneur takes root in Sid's mind.

For the next few days, Sid locks himself up in the computer lab with a mission to turn his entire presentation on its head to find the most strategic way to deliver his message. He has to start afresh, from scratch. He skips all the parties and celebrations, and eats his food at odd hours so that he doesn't have to waste time socializing.

Obviously, Anjali notices this. On a Saturday evening, when they are out for dinner, she asks, "Is everything alright, Sid? You seem very lost, very distracted."

"Yes, everything is alright," Sid says. He holds Anjali's hand from across the table.

"You do know that you're the only one in our ENTIRE batch who is nowhere close to getting a job?"

"Maybe. I don't particularly care," Sid says.

"What? How can you not care about your future?" Anjali asks in an irritated tone.

"I didn't say that. I care about my future but I don't care about any job."

"Then what are you going to do?"

"I don't know."

"You are just trying to evade. We have known each other for a couple of years now. I am very familiar with your tactics."

"No seriously, I don't know what I am going to do. All I know is I don't feel like taking up a campus job."

"Then what are you going to do? Post-graduation?"

"No."

"Has any company offered you a job?"

"No."

"Then? You need to tell me clearly, Sid. What you decide impacts me, too!"

"Maybe I will start a company of my own."

"Really? And, what will that company do?"

"Digital Advertising. Based on the the findings of my project."

"Sid, are you out of your mind? It was just a final-year project. Nobody dedicates their life to a final-year project. You scored excellent grades on your project. Who cares what that Zen Advertising company thinks? Just take the grades and move on."

"Sorry, I don't think about the project this way. I am really passionate about this."

"I am not saying you shouldn't, Sid. You should be. But preserve the passion. Go to the market and learn about how it works. Get some experience under your belt. Let us save some money then you jump into it."

"Have you ever seen anyone jumping out of a cushy job to be an entrepreneur? Salary is addictive. Once we start getting fat salaries, we will go out there, buy more things, put them on EMI, and then it is impossible to come out of it."

"Maybe what you are saying is true. But you can break the mold. You can be the pioneer."

"I don't think that will work."

"Why not?"

Sid knows this is the start of a long, heated argument. He is not up to it. He tries to avoid the argument. "Let's not argue, baby. Look around you! We're at such a nice place to celebrate your success."

"My success? My foot! You haven't asked me one question about my interviews over the past few weeks. You have no idea what I went through, how I prepared, how stressed I was. You don't know anything!"

"Exactly. Let's talk about it! I am all ears. At your service. Ready to listen to every detail."

This feeble attempt is too little, too late.

They are interrupted by the waiter bringing their food and they eat most of their meal in silence.

Sid hires an auto without haggling. The auto ride back is also silent.

At the hostel gate, they just say goodnight to each other. No hugs, no kisses.

Over the next few days, Sid not only continues to edit his presentation but also contacts ad agencies to pitch his revised presentation. He discovers that it is quite a closed community. Many companies have heard about his fiasco at Zen Advertising and are quite reluctant to give him an audience. Sid's conviction in his new presentation keeps him going though, and he is determined to get an audience with one of the companies.

Finally, he makes a breakthrough. Urjaa Advertising, an upcoming ad agency, is willing to listen to his ideas. Their General Manager, Praveen Kumar, gives him an appointment. Sid is thrilled. None of his project mates want to go with him—for one, they already have a job, and for another, lambs don't usually saunter into slaughterhouses voluntarily. To them, this project is a means to an end—the cushy job. For Sid, this is a passion. He does not know how far he's going to go with this, but with the idea of a new company gnawing into his brain, he just wants to follow his instincts, take a leap, and see where he lands.

Sid reaches Urjaa advertising by himself, nearly bursting with excitement—very different from how he felt before his presentation at Zen advertising. This company is a much smaller outfit compared to Zen Advertising. The receptionist is a busy lady, doubling up as everyone's secretary and office manager. She hurriedly ushers Sid into a small meeting room and totters out for the next item on what would be a long list. A few minutes later, Praveen, the general manager, walks in.

Praveen is about five feet seven inches tall and is a spectacled, energetic person. Sid estimates that he could be in his early forties. Sid stands up and shakes his hand. Sid introduces himself, "Sir, I am Siddharth Sharma from the Indian Institute of Management, PGDBM program, 1998 batch. I have completed a project on digital advertising in India and have found some interesting trends which I would like to share with you."

Praveen nods and asks, "Are you originally from Bangalore, Siddharth?"

Sid is surprised by this question and Praveen's interest in his personal background.

Is he trying to recruit me? he thinks.

Sid says, "You can call me Sid, sir. I am from North India. My parents lived in Lucknow. I completed my schooling in Lucknow and graduation in Delhi. My parents still can't understand the difference between Bangalore and Madras. For them, everything below Bombay is Madras."

It is a feeble attempt at a joke, and understandably, Praveen does not smile.

Praveen says, "Understandable, Siddharth. People from South India can't distinguish between UP and Haryana either. We live in a strange country."

24

Sid notices that Praveen has completely ignored his request to call him Sid. Sid takes his statement as a cue to begin his presentation.

"I agree, sir, that we live in a strange country, a country where it is extremely difficult to spot upcoming trends. Currently, hundreds of crores of rupees are being spent on conventional media such as TV, newspapers, and hoardings. But perhaps we need to look at more than just this."

Praveen leans forward but any changes in his expressions are imperceptible.

Sid talks for about forty-five minutes. His words are eloquent, and his energy is infectiously enthusiastic. He ends his presentation with, "According to this study, today's youth have very different media habits, and are more interested in non-conventional media. They don't look at hoardings when they are on the road. They don't read newspapers like their parents and they don't like the TV serials their parents watch. A detailed study is required if we want to reach out to them. Maybe it is still possible that conventional media is most effective, or maybe there is a faster, cheaper, and more effective path out there through another kind of media."

Sid does not make the same mistake he did before with cocky doomsday predictions. He balances being cautiously optimistic with staying open-ended. He leaves room for further deliberations on the same topic. It works like a charm. Praveen seems receptive.

Praveen clears his throat and says, "This is very impressive, Siddharth. But our realities are different. We are still penetrating deeper into regional TV, and vernacular newspapers. New roads are being built; car and truck sales are increasing, bringing more eyeballs onto the street. It is very hard to imagine right now that these established media may not work."

Sid argues, "That may be true today, but what about tomorrow? Are you sure the same trend will continue? Isn't it prudent to assume that global trends will catch up with India, too?"

Praveen nods. "You are absolutely right. One day they will catch on. One day it is possible that conventional media may no longer be relevant."

Sid says, "So are you saying that nothing can be done right now? Now that we have spotted this trend, should I just ignore it? Or should I do something about it?"

Praveen says, "Oh, definitely you should do something about it. But unfortunately, a company like ours can't do anything about this yet."

Sid is a little disappointed. An affirmation from Praveen is good but what can the next step be?

He musters some courage and asks, "Can you help me?"

Praveen leans back in his chair, runs his fingers through his hair, thinks for a while, and says, "I think yes. I think I can connect you to someone who may be interested in this idea. But this is strictly outside Urjaa."

Excited, Sid replies, "That would be amazing! When can you connect me? I am in a bit of a rush. If nothing works out here, I need to start searching for a job."

Praveen starts looking at his mobile phone. It's a brand new Nokia model which he is clearly proud of. He dials a number and says, "Yeah, it's me. I am sending a Siddharth Sharma to meet you. He has some interesting ideas. Listen to him and call me once you are done."

Sid starts to feel butterflies in his stomach.

"When should he meet you? Oh great. I will ask him to be there."

He looks at Sid and smiles. "Cosmopolitan Club, Jayanagar, 4th block. Tomorrow. 6 p.m. Be there. Ask for Paul Verghese."

"Sure. Who is he?"

"He is a friend of mine. He is looking to invest in new companies."

Sid is beyond exhilarated and bursting at the seams with a million questions. But before he can even blurt out one, Praveen looks at his watch, gets up, shakes Sid's hand, and sends him off with a firm, "All the best! Hope it works out for you."

Sid tosses and turns that night. He doesn't know what to expect or how he should prepare well. But the fact that someone took an interest in his idea and asked him to meet an investor is good enough for him at this stage. He starts running through his mental checklist. The presentation is ready. He has ironed the shirt and trousers he wants to wear. He has borrowed a nice tie. He is going to polish his shoes just after lunch. His certificate file is ready. Still he can't help but think that something is missing.

That is when he thinks about what led him to a breakthrough last time—the Akbar-Birbal Stories. He sits up, reaches out for the book, and starts with the first story.

The World Discovers Birbal

Once Akbar Badshah, the ruler of India in the twelfth century, went hunting. He spotted a deer and started chasing it on horseback. The deer was fast and nimble. Badshah chased it for a while, but it disappeared somewhere in the forest. Now Badshah and his army were disoriented, and lost in the forest. It was getting dark and Badshah wanted to go home. While wandering around in the forest, they saw a boy, about 10–12 years old. Akbar Badshah asked him, "Hey boy, does this road go to Agra to the big royal palace?"

The boy raises an eyebrow and remarks, "This road doesn't go anywhere. The road stays here, but if you go down this road, you will reach Agra, your royal palace."

His witty remark made Akbar Badshah laugh. But his soldiers were upset. They said, "Hey boy! Speak properly. Do you know who you are talking to?"

He said, "Yes, I do. He is Akbar Badshah, the ruler of India."

"Then how dare you talk to him like that? He's the most powerful man in the country."

The boy smirks, "But he is lost right now and not even his big army can help him find his way home. He needs my help, which makes me more powerful than him."

This made the Badshah laugh even harder.

Ultimately, the boy helped Akbar and his army find their way back.

Akbar told the commander, "I want you to keep track of this boy. Once he grows up, I will employ him in my court as an advisor."

The commander says, "I beg your pardon, Badshah. Why do you want to employ such a rude boy who doesn't know how to talk to you with respect?"

Akbar says with a smile, "He's not rude, he's intelligent, witty, and fearless. He is Birbal."

This is how the world discovered Birbal.

He puts the book down and decides to try sleeping again. Could it be a big day tomorrow?

Sid has never been to any club before. Cosmopolitan Club is one of the oldest clubs in Bangalore. It has that old-world, colonial charm. The receptionist counter is made of teak wood, which was overdue for varnishing. Behind the receptionist, there is a big round clock, and some paintings of people whom he could not identify. He is here to see Paul, the angel investor recommended by Praveen. He rushes to the receptionist and asks for Paul. She points him toward an open-air café facing the stadium.

Paul looks exactly like what Sid imagined—a dark-skinned, plump man sporting a bristly moustache with oily hair curled back. He is wearing a cream-colored half-shirt and sipping whiskey.

Sid walks up to him and says, "Good evening, sir! My name is Siddharth Sharma."

Paul gives Sid's hand a strong shake and says, "Nice to meet you, young man. Call me Paul. I am not used to being addressed as Sir."

"In that case, please call me Sid."

Never has Sid met a more affable man. Sid sits in a chair opposite Paul.

"Would you like a drink?"

"No, sir."

"You can have it with me, young man. Booze is really cheap here. That is why I come here every day."

"No sir. I came on a bike. Even if I was okay to ride back with alcohol in my system, I don't think the police on the roads would be equally okay."

Paul laughs heartily. "You are very witty!" He bellows.

Sid's comment could be considered mildly amusing, but the alcohol in Paul's blood is amplifying the humor factor.

His comment stirs last night's Birbal story into Sid's mind. Sid knows he is smart, and now Paul thinks he is witty. He isn't sure if Birbal's qualities would help him in this situation, but he thinks there is no harm in trying. He pulls out a printed copy of his presentation, but Paul stops him.

"See Sid. I am a busy man. I don't have time to listen to your long presentation. For me, time is money."

Sid looks around. It doesn't appear as if anyone else is waiting for Paul. Paul has just ordered another drink, so he isn't going anywhere else either. How is he losing money by listening to his presentation? Sid struggles to understand.

"If you have a good idea then you should be able to explain it to me in three minutes without a presentation."

Ah, an elevator pitch!

He had recently learned this concept from their professor. A young man was looking to meet the owner of a big company to present him with an idea. He tried hard but the owner was a busy man and had no time to spare. So the young man came up with a trick. He waited near the elevator for the owner, and the minute he got to ride with him in the elevator, he pitched his idea to the owner within two minutes. His idea piques the owner's interest, and the young man gets the coveted appointment to take the discussions forward.

Their professor explains, "Every idea you want to communicate should have an elevator pitch. You should be able to communicate the most powerful ideas in less than 3 minutes."

Sid's conviction in this idea has made sure that he is ready for this challenge. He delivers his elevator pitch most eloquently and waits for Paul's reaction.

Paul keeps sipping his whiskey. Perhaps due to alcohol flowing in his bloodstream, Paul is slightly sluggish in his response. Sid is at the edge of his seat.

After a couple of minutes, Paul says, "Sounds interesting. Do you have any client who can pay?"

"No. Not yet."

"Are you confident you will get a client in three months?"

"You see, Mr Paul, it's a transformative trend. Its near-term outlook may not look very positive, but in the long run, this will be a winner," Sid tries to explain using the jargon he has learned recently.

Paul is unimpressed. "Yes or no?"

"No," says Sid, trying not to sound too despondent.

"Then what do you want?" Paul's hard-nosed financial sense was still alert in his alcohol-laden system.

"Mr Paul, this is a great idea. I am sure it is going to succeed. Please help me start a business."

Paul says, "Do you really want to start a business? Then you need to take risks and make them work. Can you do that fearlessly?"

Three words are circling in Sid's head—intelligent, witty, and fearless.

"Yes, sir. I can. If you give me a chance, I will show you I am fearless."

This time, Paul's laugh sounds like it is mocking Sid. He says, "You already showed me you aren't willing to take risks—I offered you a drink, and you told me you're afraid of the cops."

"No sir. I am not scared."

"Then can you have a large peg of whiskey right now?"

"Yes sir!" Sid has no choice.

Paul signals to the waiter. He says, "Get a Black Label peg for this boy. Make it a *Patiala*."

"What is a Patiala, sir?"

"You'll see." Paul chuckles, almost a little menacingly.

The waiter comes back with a glass half filled with whiskey.

"This is a 90 ml peg of whiskey. Can you drink it on the rocks?"

"Yes sir!" Sid is desperate.

Sid's first sip produces a burning sensation that extends from his throat to his stomach. The foul liquid literally traces the path of his food pipe. Sid isn't really a drinker—he has had a few beers but never a hard drink like whiskey.

Paul laughs again at the look on Sid's face. Sid is challenged. He starts sipping it faster, constantly checking if he is feeling drunk. Sid is sipping whiskey and trying to concentrate on Paul's story. Paul starts telling him about his retirement plan. He tells Sid that he plans to return to Kerala and live peacefully in his tea estate bungalow near Munnar. Sid learns that Paul worked for a trading company and retired recently. He has already made investments to secure a worry-free retired life. So, he was planning to invest the lump sum money he got on his retirement in a small company.

Sid had imagined Paul to be a seasoned, hard-nosed investor, but Paul turned out to be an enthusiastic angel investor. He doesn't plan to get involved in the company but expects to receive an annual dividend after the company starts earning. His lawyers, however, have warned him not to be too generous with the stake he offers to other partners.

While Paul rambles on, Sid gets a sinking feeling in his mind that this is going nowhere for his business idea. He thinks Paul is a lonely man opening up in front of an accidentally willing unknown youth over a peg of whiskey. As alcohol rushes through his bloodstream, he starts to feel more relaxed. He pretends to listen to Paul and nods occasionally, but his mind wanders.

He starts thinking about Anjali.

He first noticed her on the train he took to Bangalore. She was friendly and enthusiastic. She had started the conversation first. Later, they shared each other's lunchbox. On that long train journey, they sat together on the footboard near the door watching green fields passing by. They made jokes, and waved at farmers working in the fields and the giggling school children strolling home. Anjali had a new iPod with earphones—she shared one side with Sid, and both listened to some Hindi music as the train chugged along the tracks. It was a blissful, heartwarming journey. A starry-eyed young couple was moving toward a bright future.

When they entered the campus, they became the nucleus of their group. Delnaz, the hottest girl on the campus, was also part of their group. She had a crush on Sid. She pursued him relentlessly but Sid didn't reciprocate her feelings. He liked Anjali but never showed any signs of it. The campus was a abuzz with love stories of Delnaz and Sid, but Sid ignored them and focused on studies instead. Anjali was completely focused on her studies and assignments; never really focused on her emotions.

Things changed when they went home during the term break. After being used to each other for so long on campus, both Anjali and Sid started missing each other. They started calling from STD booths. Anjali even dropped a letter to Sid at his hostel address as a surprise. After the term break, when they met again, they made love for the first time. Soon, the news broke out on the campus. The gossip about love stories of Delnaz and Sid were quickly replaced by Anjali and Sid's love stories. Delnaz was totally heartbroken. Some said she went in depression, some said she was discouraged to continue with the course due to her poor grades. But in any case, she took a break in the next semester. She was out of picture and soon enough everyone forgot about her. Both Anjali and Sid didn't want any distractions from their studies and grades, so that they would stay focused on assignments and exams for the whole week. But Saturday evening was reserved for date nights. It would start early in the evening and sometimes end at lunchtime on Sunday. They would talk incessantly, sharing every insecurity, every happy moment, and every little thing.

This seemed to end the day Sid decided to buy that Birbal book. Anjali was distraught. Sid did take her out on a bike ride the next day to Ramnagaram—a nondescript town between Bangalore and Mysore where the 1970s legendary Hindi film *Sholay* was shot. They had a lot of fun, and Anjali accepted his apology. But Sid couldn't help but think that things were not the same anymore. Since that day, it felt like she thought she was a second priority for him, and nothing he did could alleviate that feeling. The sad thing was, he didn't know what he was feeling either.

All this is running in Sid's head as he nods mindlessly to the tune of Paul's words.

As both of them finish their drinks, Paul stops talking. Both of them don't say anything for a while. Sid doesn't know whether to stay or leave. It starts to get a little awkward.

Thankfully, after this long pause, Paul suddenly says, "I like you, Sid. Having this whiskey with me was kind of like a challenge in my head. I wanted to see if you are ready to take risks. That is very essential for business. I know they teach you how to talk at your MBA class. I wanted to see if you can listen. I purposely told you my story, which may not be very interesting, but you listened very well."

Sid tries to maintain a straight face.

Paul continues, "You are smart, you are witty, you are bold. I will help you. See me tomorrow at the Domlur Post office at 6 p.m."

Paul waves at the waiter and prepares to leave.

Sid doesn't know what help Paul means. But he is ready to take whatever he can get and is elated at the progress. He decides to take the risk-taking attitude all the way. He decides to ride back on his bike instead of taking an auto. He does not want to haggle and spoil his mood. He just wants to meet Anjali and tell her everything.

***

It is the same Paul who has sent the email to fire Sid from the company. The relationship between Paul and Sid has turned on its head in a decade.

CHAPTER 2

Climbing the Ladder

Worry about the direction, not the speed.

May 2006

Sid is riding his bike behind Paul's car through a maze of small lanes in Domlur. Paul has promised to show Sid his apartment—a proposed office space for the company. Paul has agreed to be an angel investor and Sid is the person in charge of running the company, without any interference from Paul. This agreement seems to suit them both.

All Paul wants to do is go back to Kerala and enjoy his retirement. Until recently, Paul was working in an advertisement agency called MLM Creatives. This is a small outfit and holds no candle to other bigger agencies such as Urjaa Advertising Agency or Zen Advertising Agency. A few years before he retired, Paul had applied for a copywriter's position at Urjaa. Praveen had interviewed him. Although Paul didn't get the job, they kept in touch.

After retirement, he meets Praveen over a coffee. Praveen is a man of thousands of interests. Perhaps his success in life can be attributed to him keeping in touch with people from many different walks of life. He is curious why Paul wants to meet him so he just goes with the flow. Paul, perhaps like many Keralites, is bodily present in Bangalore, but his mind is always thinking about Kerala. From his savings, he has bought a small plot in a tea garden, which is now rented to a local tea company and fetches handsome returns. He has bought a couple of properties which are rented out.

Earlier he had a fleet of five auto rickshaws, which later he upgraded to two Mahindra Boleros, which are rented out to local transporters and fetch regular rental. He also has a small shop that serves as a neighborhood *Kirana* cum photocopy shop. Basically, through his meagre salary, he had saved enough to ensure a happy and relaxed retirement.

But as they say, life is all about achieving the next level.

In his social circle in Kerala, he always brags about being in the glamorous field of advertisement. Every time he meets his friends, he shares a story or two about how they came up with some creative twist, etc. It didn't matter that as a copywriter, he was merely present in the room where the presentation happened. He would claim the glory without any hesitation. So he is the 'Mr Happening' of the group.

His close friends (pulling his leg) warn him that if he cuts off all his ties with the advertisement world and returns to Kerala, he will lose that 'aura' around him and become just another boring old man. Paul is trying his best to avoid that. The coffee invitation to Praveen was to explore if he had some ideas to stay in touch with the advertising world without having to work. This catch-up happened before the meeting between Paul and Sid. That time, Praveen had nothing to offer, but after meeting Sid, Praveen joined the dots and made the introductions.

Paul is thrilled with the idea of becoming the owner of an

advertising agency in Bangalore. Small or big didn't matter. All that mattered were the immense bragging rights he would get. Accordingly, he doesn't plan to invest a lot in this venture. He plans to provide the bare minimum infrastructure and finances to keep the company running. He wants to be at the helm of affairs without lifting his finger. Sid seems like an ideal bet.

The agreement they reach is that Sid will run the company with complete autonomy, and Paul would provide the office space, the finances, and all the secretarial and accounting support. Paul keeps 60% of the equity, and Sid gets 40% sweat equity.

They agree to some terms to transfer the equity to Sid, and the company makes steady progress. It is a perfect marriage of convenience.

Paul has money, Sid has ideas.

Paul wants to retire in Kerala, Sid wants to work hard in Bangalore.

Sid doesn't want any interference, Paul doesn't want to interfere at all.

Paul stops in front of a four-storey apartment in a sleepy neighborhood of CV Raman Nagar. The apartment building has ten families, and Paul owns one apartment on the first level. Paul reaches into his pocket, pulls out a jangling bunch of keys, and after much struggling, finally finds one that unlocks the main door. The door doesn't budge. After a combined effort of Paul and Sid straining against the door, it finally creaks open. The apartment lets out ten-year-old air in a cough of dust. It is a dusty, dirty, unkempt apartment. There isn't enough light to see clearly despite it being daytime. Sid wonders why there is a ladder lying despondently in the corner.

Sid says, "Can we switch on the light? I can't really see much."

Sid walks around and flicks at some switches, but there are no bulbs or tube lights. He looks at Paul.

Paul smiles and like an amateur David Copperfield, pulls out a bulb from his pocket with a flourish. He takes the ladder lying in the corner and slowly climbs up to reach a socket, in which he fits in the bulb.

"OK! Now you can press the switch, Sid," he chirps.

The room is suddenly filled with light.

It is a single-bedroom flat. The living room has a small balcony.

Life isn't a fairy tale. Dreams don't come true by flicking a switch. Reality is raw and always looks like this. Dusty, stuffy, with broken switches and lonely ladders. You have to treat it as a canvas and paint on it.

Paul asks, "What do you think?"

Standing in the middle of the room, inhaling that stuffy air and saving his clothes from dust, Sid looks at Paul and smiles.

January 2007

In the same flat, Sid and his colleagues are clustered impatiently around a phone. They are frequently checking and refreshing their emails. After almost 365 days of relentless effort, they may soon win their first account.

Paul's flat no longer looks the same. The living room is an office space for the team, the bedroom is now the 'brainstorming room', and the kitchen has become a pantry-cum-finance area. The balcony hosts a music system, a small bar, and a couple of easy chairs. This is their thinking area. The sofa at the entrance is a sofa-cum-bed, which is used regularly as a bed during nights out. Every wall is painted in a different color. It hardly looks like an office. Sid and his team love it.

Paul also keeps aside a certain sum for the company. He says, "Sid, I was a salaried person all my life. This is all I have to spare. You have to run the company with this money. If we run out of money, either we have to close down the company, or you have to work without salary."

Sid is a cautious person. He knows that although his idea sounds exciting on paper, getting a steady income is a long ball game. He has also studied in his management course that companies don't go bankrupt because of losses but because of poor cash flow. So, he conserves cash from day one.

As an extra favor, Paul also asks one of his friends to provide a quotation for refurbishing the flat. Sid reckons that refurbishing the flat means losing a big part of the seed capital provided. He decides against it.

Why should the office have cubicles? Why should the work table be rectangular? Why should you have expensive office chairs? Why should you have cabins and large conference rooms?

Adversity always makes you think out of the box.

Sid gets the flat cleaned and locks it. His priority is to get the team. He knows that for this maverick concept, he needs people with an open mind. He needs a young, energetic, talented bunch that is ready to break the rules. He is always intrigued about all the company names that end with the word 'limited'. So he decides to break that rule, too. He names his company 'Creativity Unlimited.' True to the name, he wants to showcase creativity in every aspect of his company. It has to be the voice of the company, an image they will abide by. Not just what the client sees but the entire way in which they conduct business.

He visits many local colleges to recruit his team. He notices that most of the companies wanting to recruit the best talent are fighting to get a chance to recruit students on day one of the placement season. He decides to break this rule, too. He goes to each college with a request that he wants to be the last company on the campus. Most placement officers are surprised at this request.

Sid explains, "I have seen that most students recruited on day one go after big brand names and big salaries. I have nothing to offer on this front. On the other hand, those who can't secure a job till the last day are often not bad students but those who don't fit in the education system or have different ideas about their career."

The placement officer asks, "How are you so sure?"

Sid smiles and says, "I am one of them. Despite being part of such a prestigious school, I haven't secured a job on campus. I want something else from my career. I am looking for like-minded people."

In this case, this maverick strategy doesn't really seem to work. There is so much demand for talented students that almost everyone is placed within the first few days and the companies visiting the campus on the last day return empty-handed. But the one thing Sid has is patience. He enjoys giving speeches and looking at the reaction of the students when he says that he is employee number one, and he is there to recruit employee number two. It is fun to observe how different students react differently when he says that his office is an unfurnished single-bedroom flat. He argues that most major global IT companies, like Microsoft, started that way. Some starry-eyed students look at this as the coolest thing; others shrug it off as a crazy idea. Sid follows, and perfects this routine, campus after campus. Soon, he starts seeing some success.

On one of the campuses, he meets Jyotichandrika. Her biodata looks pretty ordinary. She has never failed but never secured first class, either. She has participated in many extracurricular activities like dance, singing, elocution, and squash but has never won any tournament or received any award. Also, there doesn't seem to be any pattern in the activities she has participated in.

She walks into the room for her interview.

From the name Jyotichandrika, Sid imagines that he would be meeting a traditional South Indian girl in traditional attire with a long braid, some tasteful gold jewelry and possibly a *Bhasma* on her forehead. This is the stereotype playing in his head. This could not have been further from the reality that is Jo.

She has a chic short bob, with a light-brown streak right in the center. She is wearing a white sleeveless top and a maroon-colored short skirt. She has a heart-shaped tattoo on her neck between her left cheek and ear. She is wearing gold chunky earrings and high heels. There is an air of confidence around her. She walks in, looks at Sid in his eyes, and gives a firm, professional handshake.

"Call me Jo," she says as an introduction.

Sid takes a minute or two to recover from his initial shock.

"Why not Jyotichandrika?" Sid asks teasingly in response. "Such a nice name."

"Yeah. My parents thought so, too. But I have hated my name ever since I can remember! I couldn't even say it properly till I was seven and I only remembered the spelling after I turned eleven!"

Both of them laugh. There is an instant connection.

"I never really felt like the 'Jyotichandrika' my parents wanted me to be. Ever since I was a child, I have hated anything that is traditional, from the customs, the clothes to the food. I didn't like anything. I was dying to leave Coimbatore and move to a bigger city like either Chennai or Bangalore. The first chance I got I moved here. I got my first tattoo within six months of coming here," she says while pointing at the heart-shaped tattoo on her neck.

Sid asks, "I know most South Indian girls are good at singing and dancing so that doesn't come as a surprise. But why squash? Did you know how to play it?"

Jo giggles and says, "Not at all. I didn't even know what a squash court looked like or what the rules were."

"Then?"

"The sports secretary was asking if anyone knew how to play squash. Nobody raised their hands. So I thought—well, nobody around knows this game, neither do I. So it's a great opportunity to try something new. I raised my hand." Jo giggles again.

"Did you win the tournament?"

Jo laughs aloud and says, "Yeah, totally! No, not at all. By some accident, I won the first round. I guess my opponent was also in the same category as I was. In the second round, I met an opponent who went on to win the tournament. So I didn't feel that bad about my loss."

"So if you get another chance, would you do something similar again?"

Jo says, "Hell yes! I had so much fun learning this game. It was a great time learning something new, and making new friends. I knew I was not going to win anything and I wanted to enjoy the process."

Within the first five minutes, it is clear to Sid that Jo would be a great fit for Creativity Unlimited. The rest of the interview is completed just as a formality.

In another campus interview, he meets Jeetendraprasad. He turns up for a campus interview in distressed jeans and a white round-neck T-shirt. It appears as if someone forced him to attend the interview. Boredom is written all over his face. Sid is amused. He has never met a candidate like Jeetendraprasad before.

Sid starts his questions. "So, Mr Jeetendraprasad . . . "

"Call me Jee," Jeetendraprasad interrupts him rudely.

Sid tries to hide his smile and says, "Why? Jeetendraprasad is such a nice name."

Jee says, "If I call myself by that name I feel older. 'Jee' feels alive, feels like me." Sid sees the streak of rebellion that he is looking for.

"Haven't you had a conversation with your parents about this?" Sid asks.

Jee says matter-of-factly, "I don't speak to them much."

Sid is intrigued. "Why? Don't you love them?"

Jee says, "I do love them, but they seem to love only Jeetendraprasad, not Jee. So, I feel they haven't accepted me for who I am."

"Interesting."

Patient active listening by Sid opens Jee up.

"In my second year of college, I moved out and rented a shared flat close to the college. I visit my parents only on weekends."

Sid says, "That is ok. Even I started staying on my own ever since I joined college."

"I wouldn't think your parents live in the same town, do they? For Bangalore this is not very common. My parents were heavily criticized by all our relatives. But I don't care much."

"Don't you miss home food?"

"No. Not at all. In fact, one of the reasons I stayed away was because I hate homemade. I like western food. My family is vegetarian, but I like chicken, fish, mutton. . . everything."

Sid asks him a few more questions about his academics and extra-curricular activities, but decides to hire him for that little streak of rebellion and the courage he has shown to be his person. Jee is his second recruit after Jo.

He recruits four more colleagues and brings them all to Paul's flat. They are surprised to see that it is unfurnished.

Sid says, "As you heard in my talk, I want everything about Creativity Unlimited to be different. So I offer you this empty, unfurnished flat. As my first batch of recruits, you can choose what it should look like."

Jo looks around and says, "This is a cool idea. I have always hated offices that have cubicles, and you have to sit in an office chair. I love my bean bag. I would be most comfortable working in that."

Sid says, "Cool. Please bring your bean bag to the office and you can use it in lieu of your official desk. The rest of you can bring whatever you want."

Jee says, "My uncle is about to discard a sofa-cum-bed in their house. It's one of my favorite things about his house. Maybe I will ask him to give it to me, and I will put it right here, next to this wall."

The office seating is sorted without Sid having to shell out any money.

Then they discuss wall paints. Raj is a graffiti artist. He offers to do the walls in colors and graffiti of their choice. Some want their corner orange, some paint it burgundy, some paint it turquoise blue. The office looks more like a studio than an office.

Ideas start flowing in. Soon the single-bedroom flat gets converted to the coolest office in town. On Fridays, the balcony also doubles up as a party space. They get some beer, buy cheap snacks, play nice music, order pizza, and dance till they drop. Those who don't want to go home, use Jee's sofa-cum-bed to sleep there.

On weekdays, they work twice as hard. They brainstorm to come up with the most creative ideas for pitches, challenge each other without a second thought, and argue passionately, because they always put the work first and try to give their best.

Although Sid is the boss, he has deliberately initiated a culture where everyone has an equal say. There is no hierarchy, no chain of command and nobody is afraid to tell him what they are thinking. The idea of nicknames is strongly entrenched in the culture post his interview with Jo, so everyone who joins Creativity Unlimited gets a nickname of their choice. Sid also asks them to call each other 'buddies' rather than 'coworkers' or 'staff'. He argues that a buddy is someone who watches your back in difficult times. If Creativity Unlimited has to be successful, he needs this attitude deeply embedded in everyone.

Sid steadily builds a work-hard, party-hard culture.

These recruits and Sid are now sitting at the center of the working area, around the phone with bated breath. Sid had his first meeting a few months ago with the MD of Orchid Advertising Agency. He wanted to offer them digital advertising and marketing services for their clients.

Sid reaches the office and walks up to the receptionist. She is busy talking on the phone. In his excitement, he doesn't wait for her to hang up and says loudly, "I am here to see Mr Gupta."

With a look of mild annoyance, the receptionist signals toward the conference room.

He knocks and enters. Mr Gupta is waiting for him. He asks him to sit down and starts looking through his papers. "Mr Sharma, when did you pass out of your college?" Mr Gupta asks in a curt voice.

Sid didn't expect this question to start the conversation.

"Sir, I passed out last year."

"So, what were you doing till now? Why didn't you find a job?"

Sid is puzzled still. "Well, I was trying to start my own business."

"Oh, I see! What kind of business? It must be funded by your father or rich uncle."

"Excuse me, sir?"

"I know today's generation. They despise hard work. They just want to take advantage of their father's finances and delay getting to the grind. Right, Mr Sharma?" Mr Gupta glowers at him over his glasses expectantly.

Sid is taken aback. He calms himself and clears his throat. "Sir, I am not sure what you are talking about. My father is not rich, and I don't have any rich uncles either. I've built my company myself, and I have come here to discuss a business concept with you. It is okay if you are not interested, but you are really not in any position to judge me."

Sid can't hide his irritation.

Mr Gupta looks taken aback, like he is also missing something. He looks at his paper and looks at Sid. "You are Nikhil Sharma, applying for an office executive position, right?"

"No sir. I am Siddharth Sharma from Creativity Unlimited. I have come here to explain the digital advertising and marketing service our company wants to offer you."

"Oh! I am sorry for the mix-up. I was expecting Nikhil Sharma. He is a candidate for the office executive position."

"No worries," says Sid, relieved on the inside.

"Let us go to my cabin and continue our discussion." Mr Gupta needs a breather to get out of the embarrassing situation. "I have heard a lot about you and your digital marketing theory from Paul. It would be interesting to listen to you."

Gupta takes him to his cabin. On his way, he has a heated, hushed discussion with the receptionist, probably blaming her for the mix-up. He asks her to send coffee for Sid in his cabin.

To get over the embarrassing start, Gupta indulges in small talk. "So what is your hometown, Siddharth?"

"You can call me Sid. I belong to Lucknow."

"How long have you been in Bangalore? How do your parents feel about you being here so far away?"

"I got into IIM Bangalore and decided to come to here. My parents were totally against this. They haven't really been to the south side of India much; they come from the generation that thinks that everything south of Bombay is 'Madras'. They also

46

think that in 'Madras', you get only rice and nobody has heard of paneer. It's pretty ridiculous."

"So how did you convince them?"

"It was not easy for sure. But that is what mothers are for. My mother still doesn't understand what I study or my career is. But back then, she knew that I wanted to do this desperately. So she convinced my father, and here I am."

"Indeed. Between you and me, Sid, my story won't sound too different," said Mr Gupta.

Light laughter provides a good transition between small talk and shop talk.

"So Sid, what is this new advertising idea that you are talking about?"

"Well, sir. I did my project work on new and upcoming ideas in advertising and I made some shocking observations. The new upcoming technology is going to change everything we do sir, including how we communicate with the customers."

"Do you have any basis to say that?"

"Yes, sir." Sid tries to pull out his laptop to show the same presentation he has been making over and over again.

Gupta stops him and says, "No, I don't want to listen to your presentation. Please tell me in one minute why you think so."

"Oh, an elevator pitch?"

"Yes. You are aware of this concept?"

"Of course," Sid says, and he thanks Paul in his mind.

"Go ahead. Your time starts now."

It is indeed a trial by fire for Sid.

Sid clears his throat and says, "Today's youth is the biggest draw for any marketer in India. We define this group as those born in the late 80s and 90s, who are vastly different from their parents born in the 50s, 60s, and 70s. Their media consumption habits are totally different. They don't read newspapers, they don't notice large billboards and they hate prime-time TV serials. So all the advertising money that you pour in to reach them is wasted. My company, Creativity Unlimited, has been established to help companies target young customers by choosing the appropriate media, tone, and mode of communication. The budget we need at this stage is a small fraction of the total budget, but we are sure it is totally worth its value."

There is a long, awkward pause after Sid completes. Sid can't help but feel that it came out much better than he expected. Gupta is impressed but maintains a poker face.

"You . . . have an interesting theory, Sid. Have you proved it anywhere?"

"No sir. We are in the initial stages of propagating our concept. We have had very interesting discussions with many companies, but we don't have a case study yet."

"Fair enough. We will give you the opportunity to bid for a project. If you are good enough, you may get it. Please wait at the reception. I will request my colleague to meet you and share a project for which we are looking for partners."

"Wow! That is cool!"

Gupta doesn't like the exuberance on display. He follows up with an immediate dampener.

"I don't want to raise your hopes too much, Sid. Let me put it this way. This concept is totally new. We don't even know how to evaluate it. If you present your idea very clearly and thoroughly, then and only then you have a chance."

"That is totally acceptable, sir." Sid gets up and shakes hands.

Sid meets Gupta's colleague and receives the brief for the project. The brief is very vague. All it says is—'We are working with a sports shoe brand.' They need to target young customers. They are willing to experiment and spend on new ideas. Please come up with a plan.

Sid tries to ask more questions, but he doesn't get any useful answers. Sid brings the brief back to the office to discuss it with his team. They go over it again and again, but they are unable to make any headway.

Sid says, "Let us sleep over it, guys. Let us meet tomorrow with a fresh mind to discuss this."

Jo says, "There is nothing in this brief that we are going to discover tomorrow. I think it is a dead end. They have set us up on a path of failure."

"Calm down. What Sid is saying is right. We will get some bright ideas tomorrow to crack this. Maybe some wise man will come in our dreams and tell us what to do," Jee says jokingly.

Nobody laughs. But this gets Sid thinking. Maybe, a wise man could indeed help? Could Birbal possibly provide some pearl of wisdom that could change the trajectory of this brief on its head? He couldn't be sure, but Birbal's tales had brought him this far, so he thought it wouldn't hurt to try again.

Sid says, "Buddies, I think I will have something by tomorrow. Jee may have tried to crack a very bad joke, but he has suddenly given me an idea that could maybe solve the problem. I will consult a wise man tonight."

Jo says, "Sid! You too! What wise man? What are you saying?"

Sid just winks and says, "Goodnight buddies."

Sid parks the bike in a tight space earmarked for him by his landlord. He has rented a room on the first floor of a small bungalow in Indiranagar. The landlord stays on the ground floor. They are a couple in their mid-sixties, with two children living abroad. Their daughter married and left for the United States about three years ago, and their son left to do his masters in Australia a year ago. They were looking for young couples to rent out their rooms, but when Sid came to see the room for the first time, he was wearing a pink-striped shirt that was similar to their son's favorite shirt. When he expressed an interest in the room, the landlady, who was missing her son, was emotionally stirred to offer him the room on the spot.

Sid has an independent entrance to his room through a narrow staircase. It is a large room with a small kitchenette and an attached toilet. It is a comfortable, cozy home. Sid keeps odd working hours and never bothers to cook at home except for making tea on rare occasions. The landlady invites him for breakfast or lunch once in a while. Sid finds it very awkward to accept her invitations, but tasty homemade food lures him every time. When Sid visits them, they keep talking about his son and how he is missing homemade food and the comforts of his own home. Sid realizes that they see their son in him. The invitations are more to feed a void inside them.

Sid reaches his room and searches for his Birbal book. He flips through the stories until he finds a title that catches his attention.

Birbal and the Bags of Rice

One evening, Akbar and his begum were relaxing on the terrace. The begum was jealous of Birbal because he could get Akbar to do whatever he wanted. She wanted her younger brother to be the wazir instead. But Akbar was so fond of Birbal that both of them were always together. That evening, Birbal was away, so she leapt at the opportunity.

She said, "Jahanpanah, you give too much importance to that kafir Birbal. You listen to him for everything." Akbar just smiles at her.

She continues, "I don't think there is anything special about Birbal. In fact, I think my younger brother Muhammad is much smarter than Birbal. You have to make him a wazir."

Akbar said, "No, Begum. Muhammad may be more educated, but he is no match for Birbal."

Begum said, "I don't care. You must make him a wazir. Otherwise, I will be mad at you."

Akbar thought for a moment and said, "Ok. Let us give him a test. If he does better than Birbal in the test, then I will make him wazir."

Begum agreed. Akbar summoned Muhammad to the terrace. Upon his arrival, Akbar heard the creaking sound of bullock carts passing by. Small bells tied around the bullocks were making a gentle tinkling sound.

Akbar looked at Muhammad and said, "Please find out what that sound is all about?"

Muhammad glanced over and said, "Some bullock carts are passing by."

Akbar asked, "How many of them?"

Muhammad ran down, quickly counted them, and rushed back.

"Jahanpanah, there are 12 bullock carts," he said breathlessly.

Akbar asked, "What are they carrying?"

Muhammad realized he did not know and ran back again to ask. He came back panting and said, "They are carrying rice, Jahanpanah."

Akbar asked, "Where are they coming from?"

Again, Muhammad ran to the carts and came back with the information, "They are coming from Azizpur, a village near the Yamuna River." Muhammad desperately hoped this was enough information.

Then Akbar, with a hand on his chin, asked, "Where are they going?"

With a deep breath, Muhammad ran back to the carts, which were slowly moving further and further away.

He needed a minute to catch his breath. "Jahanpanah, they are going to Rajasthan, and I don't think if you ask me anything more, I can catch up with them."

Then Akbar summoned Birbal.

He said to Birbal, "We heard some sound on the streets some time back. Can you find out what the sound all about?" To be fair to both, he asked exactly the same question to Birbal as he had to Muhammad.

Birbal nods, leaves and takes a while to come back. The Begum and Muhammad are overjoyed.

But Birbal returned after an hour. He looked at Akbar, bowed and said, "Jahanpanah, I traced the sound to some bullock carts that were passing by. There were about twelve bullock carts going from Azizpur to Jaipur. They were carrying rice. I checked the sample of their rice and asked them for the price. I was surprised to find that their rice quality is much better than ours and the price is also reasonable. So I have asked them to stay in our palace quarters tonight. Let us meet them in court tomorrow and purchase their rice and make the payment."

The Begum and Muhammad realized their mistake and quietly left.

Sid is so taken in by the story that he reads it four more times.

He can't help but think that this story directly applies to the problem he has on hand. The request for proposal provided by the client asks a question as vague as the question Akbar asks in the story. But Birbal goes above and beyond to find out everything that needs to be known and that's how he wins. He also considers a possibility that Akbar didn't really know what he was looking for but it was Birbal who defined it for him and made the entire question meaningful.

Sid decides to follow the learnings from Birbal's story yet again to solve his problem. Instead of just providing an obvious answer to the question, he needs to ask more questions like "Where is the flock of bullock carts going?"; "Why are they going there?"; etc. In short, Birbal didn't take Akbar's question at face value. He went into depth and found out everything that could have been known about the bullock carts. Although Akbar's question was unclear, he could come up with a comprehensive solution, which probably Akbar also didn't know he needed.

Sid realizes he has to do just that.

The client just asked, 'What should we do to launch a sports brand for youth'. Rather than just answering the question on its face value, Sid decides to apply Birbal's technique by breaking down the main question in several sub-questions, find the answers to them and then roll up all the answers to create a comprehensive answer to the original question. That would make the exercise meaningful. First obvious question is how are the sports shoes being bought presently? What are the customers looking for? How are the salespersons fulfilling their current needs? How the shoes are being used? What are the usage patterns? What are the unmet needs? How are the competitor brands being advertised? Do the lofty claims made in the advertisements match with the user experience? Sid's mind was abuzz with so many questions, just like Birbal's mind would have been, while answering a simple question posed by the Badshah.

The next day when he meets his buddies, he kick-starts them into action. He assigns them clear tasks to get to the root of the main challenge. Jee is told to visit the shops that sell the footwear to take a look at the product, talk to the shoe salesmen to know more about the brand. He asks Jo to talk to some customers who are wearing them. He asks others to go to popular jogging spots in the morning and evening to observe joggers and identify the potential problems. He starts to watch the advertisements of their competitors from the data that he has. The whole team is focused on finding as much as they can about the brand and then looking at all the data points to come up with a pitch.

They work on putting together their proposal for five days straight. Hardly anyone goes home. The sofa-cum-bed in the office comes in handy. The Shivsagar restaurant nearby provides food delivery at no extra cost. There's even a shower in the apartment, so nobody has any hygiene concerns either. They just work day and night to ensure that their proposal is compelling. It works like magic.

Today is the day of the outcome.

Finally, the phone rings. Everyone jumps up and fights with each other to not pick up the call first. Finally, Jo snatches the phone and answers, "Hi, good afternoon, this is Creativity Unlimited.

May I help you?" All the buddies have to keep from bursting into laughter at her imitation of a professional receptionist. She also struggles to keep a straight face.

Jo continues, "Oh sure. Let me check if he is free."

She holds the phone for a few seconds to more muffled laughter and says, "He is talking to another client, would you mind holding on for a minute?"

Sid almost falls over in his attempt to get to the phone, but only grabs at the empty air as Jo twirls out of his way and expertly dodges his grabbing attempts. She obviously wants Orchid Advertising to believe that they are not the only client Sid deals with and are very busy.

After one long, impatient minute, she says, "He is free now. Let me connect you to him."

She presses the hold button again and giggles as she passes the phone to the breathless Sid, who starts speaking, "Yes . . . speaking."

"Good afternoon . . . Good . . . how are you?"

"Ahhh. . . ya. . . that's right."

"That is challenging but doable."

"We can try. We will give it our best shot."

"Okay. Okay. Talk to you soon."

He completes the conversation and keeps the phone down with a very serious face. For almost 30 seconds, everyone practically hears each other's heartbeats.

Sid smiles and shouts, "We got it, guys! We have our first client!"

Screams and spontaneous celebrations erupt. Someone shakes open a cold drink bottle and sprays everyone. Someone else blasts the music system. Paper confetti is thrown into the air. Everyone starts dancing. Handshakes. Hugs. Kisses. The air smells of success, sticky coke, and joy.

This moment is a golden memory permanently etched on everyone's mind.

CHAPTER 3

Trouble in Paradise

Good Samaritans aren't always angels.

February 2012

After their first order from Orchid Advertising agency, there was no looking back.

Creativity Unlimited grows rapidly. Until the year 2010, their strategy is to work with ad agencies, PR agencies, and brand agencies to create digital campaigns for their clients. Clients would spend crores with the ad agencies, out of which a few lakhs would be diverted to Creativity Unlimited. That small fraction of the client's budget is good enough for Creativity Unlimited to thrive. They prefer to deal only with ad agencies and not directly with their clients.

In many cases, the clients like car companies, fast-moving consumer goods companies don't even know that the campaigns are being worked on by Creativity Unlimited. This suits everyone. The ad agencies can convince the clients to divert some money to the digital medium, at the same time, they are not losing control of the outflow.

Sid is happy because Creativity Unlimited is not big enough to approach all clients spread across India. They can deal with a few progressive ad agencies and grow their business.

The business is great, the team is growing, and cash registers are ringing. Sid is busy as hell, hence happy. Paul is enjoying his life in Kerala. He is getting decent money as well as a load full of bragging rights from Creativity Unlimited.

The year 2009 was the inflection point. By then, Creativity Unlimited was seen as a rising star in the field of advertising. Sid and his team came up with some brilliant campaigns for Orchid Advertising and other clients, which didn't go unnoticed. There was a beeline of clients. To cope with the demand, Sid had to recruit new buddies as fast as he could.

Sid wanted to attract the right talent and provide them with the right working environment. He devised his own maverick way to recruit the right talent. Even today, he would follow the same practices.

He chooses a handful of colleges where he would recruit. These are not the top-notch colleges but are known for all round development of students rather than just academics. He looks for students who have shown some originality or out-of-the-box thinking rather than better grades. He also prefers rebellions over conformists.

To attract and retain talent, Sid has devised liberal human resource strategies. These strategies are the opposite of practices followed by other companies. First and foremost, at Creativity Unlimited, salary is not confidential information. He has created an internal portal where everyone's salary, including Sid's own salary, is displayed. Sid argues that this ensures that there is no scope for rumors. The gossips about salary disparity is the main bone of contention in most of the other companies. Sid nips this in the bud.

Secondly, there is no hierarchy and no lofty designations. Everyone is called a buddy internally, and externally, they are known as a Team Leader or Team Member. The team leader and team member are interchangeable. A team leader for one project may be a team member for another, and vice versa. This fosters team spirit and equitable relationships.

Sid also has the most liberal attendance and leave policies. There is no fixed start and end time for the office. Each buddy can choose the working time that suits them. Nobody keeps track of attendance, or the number of hours spent in the office. As long as the work is done, buddies are free to come and go whenever they please.

This freedom makes the employees even more loyal to the work, and they end up putting in as much effort as required without once looking at their watches. The leave policy is also very unique. Buddies have unlimited leaves in a year. They can avail of it whenever they want, with only one condition. They inform all the team leaders and team members they are working with, and if they are traveling for a vacation, they have to post all their pictures and travelogues in an internal portal. This ensures that there is no taboo associated with going on vacations, and transparency ensures that the work doesn't suffer.

All of these policies work to Sid's advantage. Soon the word spreads and Creativity Unlimited starts getting a cult following among some students. Since Creativity Unlimited was the last company to visit the campus, these students wait until the last day to accept offers from other companies. Despite the low salary offered by Creativity Unlimited, it has become a coveted employer in India.

In 2009, they run out of space in Paul's one-bedroom apartment and move to a brand-new office nearby. Paul takes out a bank loan and invests in a new office. Sid insists on retaining their unique way of doing up the office, without cubicles, fixed desks, and dull colors on the wall.

As a result, the office retains the unique look. No desks, office chairs, or cubicles. Only bean bags, easy chairs, and sofas. The walls are painted rich shades of burgundy, turquoise blue, and maroon.

On the business front, Sid's strategies have also worked well. After the first contract from Orchid Advertising, there was no turning back. Working with Orchid gave them name and fame. Soon, most other advertising companies hire Creativity Unlimited for digital media work.

By the year 2011, they were working with many advertising companies except for a few. Urjaa Advertising, where Praveen worked, is one of them. It was quite ironic that Praveen was instrumental in connecting Paul and Sid, which started Creativity Unlimited, but he hadn't met both of them ever since.

Sid wants to meet and say thank you, but Praveen isn't available. Sid wants to pitch his digital media solution to Urjaa, but he is blocked. Praveen was a General Manager when Sid met him in 2006. He quickly climbed the corporate ladder and became the Vice President of Urjaa by the year 2012. He was also rumored to become the next CEO of Urjaa in a few years. He is considered one of the most respected personalities in the field of advertising.

Sid, however, has a vastly different experience dealing with him. Sid makes numerous attempts to meet him, but Praveen always pretends to be occupied with other engagements. Paul also wants to connect, but Praveen dodges him too. Sid is puzzled by this behavior as he can't possibly assign any reason or rationale. But he moves on.

By 2011, Creativity Unlimited has earned its name. They are the secret weapon for most of the advertising agencies. They are also one of the most preferred employers in India.

When the new financial year starts in 2012, Sid is looking to grow his business further. Creativity Unlimited is getting steady business from most of the advertisement agencies. To grow his business, he needs new clients. After intense brainstorming with his team, they decide that the time has come to directly approach clients of advertising agencies and ask for business. This strategy has many advantages.

Firstly, large companies with bigger budgets would know Creativity Unlimited directly, so they would get higher budgets. Secondly, most of the work they do is used by advertising agencies under their name. So, the public in general doesn't know about Creativity Unlimited. However, this strategy has a lot of risks, too. If they bypass the advertising agencies and go directly to their clients, they may stop giving work to Creativity Unlimited.

Secondly, managing clients directly is a different ballgame altogether and Sid is not sure if his culture is well suited for that. After a lot of deliberation, they decide to go after clients of advertising agencies who are not working with them. In that way, there is no conflict of interest, and they will get to test the waters.

In January 2012, Sid set up a meeting with Apex Computers Ltd. They are India's leading computer and laptop assemblers. Their research indicates that Apex is trying to target young customers with their latest products. Apex has launched a funky-looking computers and laptops to attract young adults. Targeting young customers successfully is the core competency of Creativity Unlimited, so it looks like a natural fit.

Sid meets Mr Shroff, the owner of Apex Computers. He is a humble man, who started this company in a garage two decades ago. His struggle is similar to Sid's. They connect very well. Sid explains what they can do to grow Apex's business by increasing their appeal to younger customers. Mr Shroff hears him out but is quite reserved when it comes to committing to the next steps. Sid knows it is going to take a while for him to get any business from Apex, so he is not disheartened.

He returns to the office, very pleased with the meeting and his new strategy.

Right then, out of the blue, Sid gets a call from Praveen from Urjaa Advertising.

"Hello, Praveen."

"Hello, Siddharth, how are you?"

"I am fine, Praveen. It's been a long time since we met."

"Yes, not since I introduced you to Paul."

"That is right, Praveen. After Paul funded Creativity Unlimited, I tried to get in touch with you to thank you many times. But you were not available."

"Indeed. I got your messages, but the time was not right to see each other."

"Oh." Sid gets a confirmation that Praveen was dodging him.

Sid asks, "So, how can I help you now?"

Praveen says, "How are you doing? How is your outfit doing? I hear a lot of good things about you."

Sid is intrigued by the choice of words—'outfit'. "We are doing good. We are working with quite a few advertising agencies, and they are happy with our services. So business is good," Sid says.

"That is great to hear, Siddharth."

No matter how many times Sid asks him to call him by his nickname, Praveen insists on calling him Siddharth. Sid thinks that maybe this is his way of maintaining a formal distance in the relationship. Sid still can't figure out why Praveen has called him.

Sid says, "I tried contacting Urjaa to offer our services, but I didn't receive a positive response. I hope you got to know about our approach."

Praveen says, "Yes, of course, every single time. But as I said, the time wasn't right for us to meet and engage."

Sid says, "I see. I presume something has changed and that's why you have called me."

Praveen laughs and says, "Yes indeed. Good guess."

There is a pause in the conversation. Sid decides to hold the pause forcing Praveen to speak up.

Praveen says, "Urjaa wants to enter into a long-term contract with your company. I would like to meet you and Paul to discuss the terms."

Sid says, "Really? That is great news," Sid says but he can't hide the skepticism in his voice. He is quite intrigued by the timing of this call.

Praveen says, almost as if he is reading Sid's mind, "You might be wondering why I called now, right?"

"Right."

"Well, Siddharth, you broke the unwritten rule. You started approaching our clients."

"Oh, is Apex Computers your client?"

"Yes indeed."

"Oh wow. That was fast. I just finished the meeting an hour ago and reached the office."

"In this business, one has to keep the ear to the ground, Siddharth."

"Yes indeed. I must say I am impressed with your speed."

"I have a lucrative offer for your outfit. I would like to meet you and Paul together. When can we meet?"

Sid says, "That really is great news but why do you want Paul to be present? He doesn't make business decisions. He has left all these decisions to me."

Praveen says, "Indeed. Please don't take this as anything against you. I just thought that since I haven't met both of you since you started the company, I can take this opportunity to meet you both."

"Sure. Let me check Paul's availability," Sid says.

"That won't be necessary. My secretary can do that. I will let you know when the meeting is. Please be available."

Praveen hangs up the phone.

Sid calls out for Jo and Jee to join him. He tells them about Praveen's call.

Jo says, "This Pee-dude is the same guy who connected you with Paul, right?"

"Yes."

"It's pretty weird that he called you now. After so many years."

"Yeah, I am very surprised."

Jee says, "I think we should be happy."

"Why?" Jo is as critical as ever. "I think we should be worried."

"Look, back in school, I wanted to start a band. So at dinner time, I used to sing very loudly in the mess hall. Initially, everyone used to ignore me. After a few days, they used to laugh at me. But after a few months, the college band approached me to join them."

Jo says, "How is this story connected with the current situation?"

Jee says, "Bro, we are getting noticed. Pee-dude is trying to block us. That means we are doing very well."

Sid says, "Maybe you are right."

Although this seems like good news, Sid is not entirely happy. He thinks that there is something more to it than Praveen is saying. He finds Praveen's approach very patronizing. He keeps wondering about Praveen's insistence on Paul's presence and his direct approach to Paul. He senses trouble.

After the fateful call, he leaves his office earlier than usual. By the time he reaches home, it is 8 p.m. His landlady is very happy to see him. She has made *bisi bele bath,* a traditional Kannada dish. She calls him out and asks him to collect it on his way up. Sid feels very awkward accepting such things from her, but he knows why she is doing it. It is her son's favorite dish, so when she misses him too much, she cooks it and then insists on Sid eating it. She sends so much food that Sid no longer needs to go out for dinner.

He quickly finishes his food and lies on his bed listening to his favorite music—ghazals by Ghulam Ali. He keeps thinking about Praveen's call and tries to decipher what may be coming his way. That is when he thinks of Anjali. Anjali has a very perceptive mind. In such situations, she has always helped Sid make sense of people's behavior.

There were many situations in their business school when Sid couldn't see the ulterior motives of his friends like Delnaz or even professors when they approached him, but Anjali warned him and gave him advice that was invaluable. He misses her. He also feels guilty that he hasn't called her in a long time. He decides to make amends. He steps out and starts walking toward the nearest STD booth. The landlord has allowed him to use their phone for incoming calls, but for making outgoing calls out of state, he still has to go to the STD booth.

He takes a deep breath as the phone rings. She picks up.

"Hi, Anjali, how are you?" Sid says sheepishly.

"I am good, Sid. How are you? Is something bothering you?" Anjali says.

Sid wonders how she can read his mind being so far.

"No. Not at all. I came back early from work, and I was missing you."

"Oh really! That is very sweet of you, Sid. How are you doing?"

"Yeah, I am doing great. I work all the time, mostly, but it's fun."

Anjali says excitedly, "Hey listen, have you told everyone about your two-week leave? Our Ladakh bike trip is just three months away."

"Not yet, Anjali. But don't worry, our trip is confirmed."

"Darling, I feel most worried when you say 'don't worry'."

Both of them laugh.

"I am the boss at this place. I can do what I want," Sid boasts.

"Really, Mr Boss. Then why don't you come over and see me for Valentine's Day?" Anjali teases him.

"Oh, that weekend I have something important."

"See, I know you so well. But it's okay. Let us do this Ladakh bike trip then I will forgive you for all your mistakes."

"My mistakes?"

"*Aur nahi to kya*. You forgot to call me for so many weeks. You forgot your first-date anniversary. You didn't forget my birthday, but you called me at 11:30 p.m., thirty minutes before my birthday was over. There are many more things. Don't make me fight with you."

"Okay, baba. I have made many mistakes. But I will make up for it in Ladakh."

"Yeah. That's good. I have completed our daily plan. I have found some awesome places to visit and stay. It's going to be the vacation of our lives. I am so excited."

"Me too. How is your work? How is travel?"

"Don't ask, Sid. Travel is driving me crazy. I spent last week in Patna. It is such a crazy place. I don't know what it is; I thought everyone there was scared of each other."

"Why do you say that?"

"We had to meet a client, and we were searching for the address. We asked a person who was standing right in front of the building where we were supposed to be, and this guy sent us on a wild goose hunt. Finally, we came back to the same place after forty-five minutes."

"That is funny. How did that happen?"

"Well, the story is, I was wearing formals and I had hired a white ambassador. So everyone thought that I was an Income Tax officer or CBI officer, so nobody would tell me the correct address."

"This is hilarious," says Sid. His mind is preoccupied with Praveen but he knows he has to listen to Anjali first. That is very important for her.

Anjali went on for another ten minutes about her stories about Patna, and Sid listens patiently. Anjali says, "Okay. You listened to me very well, I feel happy. You are a good boyfriend, I miss you."

This is Sid's cue to speak up.

Sid says, "You know, a strange thing happened today."

Anjali teases him, "Now I will finally know why you called, baby! Tell me more about it."

"Do you remember Praveen?"

"The same guy who connected you to Paul and then vanished in a puff of smoke. What about him?"

"Well, he called me today. He has been dodging me on purpose for the last three to four years, and now he wants to sign a long-term contract with us. I don't get it."

"That sounds strange! I think you need to tell me his exact words."

"Well, he said that he would like to meet me and Paul together and sign a long-term deal. You know what was the strangest thing? He already initiated contact with Paul, and he insisted that he alone would make sure Paul attended."

"Why is that strange?"

"I mean, sure, he knows Paul directly, but now Paul and I are working together. He should respect that, right?"

"Yes. Technically he should. But he doesn't have to. Just think about it. He knew Paul before you so he could have contacted Paul first and then asked Paul to contact you right? But he didn't do that. He called you directly."

"Yes. That makes sense. But still, I cannot shake the feeling that he has something up his sleeve. I don't have a good feeling about this long-term deal. I can't help but think that this is a trap. But I can't figure it out."

"Yeah. It is strange for sure. It is not just a long-term deal, there is more to it than meets the eye."

"What is strange is he insists that Paul and I both should be there in the meeting. I did tell him that Paul doesn't involve himself in business-related decisions but still he insists."

"Hmm. This is interesting. I think he wants to assess how your relationship with Paul is. Whether you get along well, who has the upper hand, etc."

"But why should he bother?"

"I don't know. But my sixth sense says that he may try to drive a wedge between you two. Don't give him any gap."

"I will try."

After that, they speak for a while about other things. Sid feels validated. He walks back home with a clear mind.

***

Paul and Sid are sitting in Sid's cabin, waiting for Praveen to arrive. Paul isn't particularly proud of the unorthodox office Sid has created, so he actually wants the meeting to happen in the Jayanagar club or some hotel. But Sid insists that since it is an official discussion, it should happen in the office. Sid is afraid that, for reasons beyond his comprehension, Praveen is proposing to start the long-term relationship hastily. He welcomes the remunerative long-term relationship, but he wants it to start on a sound base. That is why Sid wants Praveen to see things as they are and minimize any mismatch in expectations.

Paul is nervous. He has no idea what to expect. His association with Praveen has been very brief and not very conclusive. He welcomes a long-term contract, but he doesn't know what the catch is. He is not quite prepared to handle it. He is also not sure why Praveen wants him to be there in the negotiations. He is trying to divert his attention to arrangements for tea and snacks. That is his way of managing his stress; instead of thinking about the actual big, pressing issue, his mind diverts to thinking about smaller, more inconsequential things and stresses over them.

Praveen enters the office.

"Very unusual office, I must say." Praveen can't hide his surprise.

"I wanted you to see this before we sign on any dotted lines," Sid fires his first salvo.

Sid continues, "In fact, I would like you to take a tour of our little office. Meet some of our buddies."

"Buddies?"

"Oh yeah. That is what we call each other in our company," Sid replies.

Sid takes Praveen around. He explains why they don't have cubicles, why the wall colors are so unusual, and why buddies are sitting on bean bags. He also shows him the entertainment room, the meditation room, the small gym and the sleeping room. To Praveen's surprise, he finds a couple of employees sleeping there at 10 a.m.

Sid says, "They must have worked through the night."

Praveen asks, "Do you monitor how much time they are spending on recreational activities?"

Sid proudly says, "No, we don't. In fact, we don't monitor their attendance either. We provide them all the freedom in the world and expect them to think creatively and deliver."

Praveen says, "That is an interesting approach." But in his mind he actually thinks of it to be an insane approach.

They get back to Sid's cabin where Paul is waiting with tea and snacks. Thambi, the silent coffee guy, serves coffee and also the samosas ordered by Paul. They chit-chat about the weather, politics, cricket, and sundry things.

Then Praveen starts to explain the purpose of his visit.

He says, "I have heard a lot about your company. I may not have spoken to you directly, but I have done my due diligence, and I am impressed with your work."

Paul says, "Thank you, sir."

Sid says, "Thank you, Praveen. That is very kind of you."

After an awkward pause, Sid says, "How can we help you now?"

Praveen says, "I have secret news to share with you. I request that you keep it confidential."

Paul and Sid nod in agreement.

Praveen clears his throat and continues, "I am slated to take over as CEO of Urjaa a few months from now. The discussions are at an advanced stage. 50% of the board members have agreed, and the other half is likely to approve my appointment very soon."

"Congratulations!" Sid says. But he is puzzled about many things. Firstly, why Praveen is entrusting them with such classified information; secondly, why is this news relevant to Creativity Unlimited?

Praveen continues, "Thank you, Siddharth. I want to chart out a new vision for Urjaa when I take over. Our current management is not forward-thinking. For example, they have not shown any inclination to work with you, have they?"

Paul asks Sid, "Have they, Sid?"

Sid knows it's a rhetorical question, so doesn't bother to answer that.

"For us to implement our new vision, digital advertising is an important part. Therefore, I want to enter into a long-term agreement with you and make sure we have that edge when we go to our clients. This will be the new face of Urjaa advertising."

Unsurprisingly, Praveen doesn't mention anything about Apex Computers in front of Paul.

Sid says, "That is great to hear. So when do we start the trial project."

Praveen says, "No, no. I don't want any trial project. I am ready to sign you on a retainer for three years."

Paul is elated. "Thank you very much, sir!"

Sid on the other hand is skeptical. "Why would you want to sign such a long engagement without a trial project?"

"Because I have done my homework. You are the most suitable partner for us."

"Still I think we should have a trial project so that our teams get to know each other well."

Paul asks, "Is that absolutely necessary?"

Sid says, "Yes, Paul. If we are entering such a long relationship, we should know what to expect. I should think about who the most suitable team leader for this would be. I need time."

Praveen says, "That is very surprising, I must say. In fact, I had brought an agreement for all of us to sign, right now. That is the reason I insisted on Paul being there."

Paul says, "Sid, I think we should go ahead."

Sid says, "No, Paul. Trust me. What I am doing is for the good of all of us."

Praveen says, "This is the first time I am experiencing this. I am ready with the agreement, but the vendor is not ready."

Paul is irritated. Sid is calm.

Praveen says, "But maybe Siddharth is right. Let us take a long-term view. Maybe we will learn about each other, and then we can work together well. Let us do what all of us are most comfortable with."

Sid asks, "Are there any clauses in the agreement we should be aware of?"

Praveen says, "Nothing much. Just the standard clause that you can't approach our clients directly."

Before Sid can say anything, Paul says, "That is quite alright."

Praveen says, "I am also proposing a retainer fee that you truly deserve. I am sure you will find the sum attractive."

The discussions are effectively concluded. Then they talk about weather, politics, and cricket again till they finish the coffee and samosas.

Praveen says, "It was nice meeting both of you. Sorry for not being available earlier. But the time must be right for everything.

I will leave the draft agreement here for both of you to review. I have already signed it. Let me know if you are okay with this."

Paul says, "Thanks!"

Sid says, "Please connect me to the engagement manager from your side so both our teams can talk to each other. Let us have a short pilot project for three months, and if everything goes smoothly, I would be happy to sign."

Praveen says, "As you wish!"

As he leaves the office, Paul says, "Let me walk you to the car."

"Thank you," says Praveen.

Walking to the car, Praveen says, "In my career of fifteen years, this is the first time that I went in with a signed agreement and returned empty-handed."

Paul says, "Personally, I am very sorry about this. I wanted to sign the agreement straight away. But since Sid runs the business, I don't want to make him upset."

"You shouldn't. I won't say he is wrong, but he definitely lacks business sense."

"Perhaps."

"Did you notice? He didn't even look at the amount. He is just bothered about pilot projects."

"Yeah, I noticed that."

"But I can see that money drives you, Paul. That is how it should be," Praveen says.

Paul tries to sound wise. "In business, that is how it should be right? If you are not going up, you are going down. If you are not making money, you are losing money."

Praveen laughs and says, "Very well said, Paul. These are wise words. Maybe you should coach Siddharth."

Paul says, "Do you think I should?"

Praveen says, "Paul, mark my words, if he continues on this path, one day, you will have to change the leader to do justice to company's potential."

Was this Praveen's foresight? Or was it his plan?

Whatever it was, it came true in 2016. Sid is asked to make way for someone else to lead Creativity Unlimited.

Sid is sitting in his cabin, wondering who he or she might be.

CHAPTER 4

The Beginning of the End

Deceptive friends are more dangerous than foes.

June 2014

Until January 2014, Creativity Unlimited's business is going smooth and easy providing digital strategies, including to Urjaa Advertising. They plan YouTube campaigns, Facebook campaigns, Twitter campaigns, and create outreach programs for established advertising agencies that focus on conventional media like televisions, newspapers, and outdoor displays. Conventional advertising agencies find this service pretty handy to fill in the gap in their portfolio.

Out of crores of rupees that were spent on TV and newspaper advertisements, a few lakhs would go to digital advertising. This is enough for a company like Creativity Unlimited. Business is growing.

Work culture sets the company apart. Work is fun, the team contributes wholeheartedly, and everyone looks forward to being at work.

Sid led this culture. He is engrossed in running Creativity Unlimited with no time for anything else. He loses touch with most of his friends. Anjali, now officially his girlfriend, finds a job in Delhi and they have an agreement to call each other at least once a week. Over the last two years, Sid has been so immersed in his work that he either forgets to call, or will not attend to her call because he is busy. His promises to call her back go unfulfilled.

The fateful Ladakh trip that he had promised would make up for his mistakes, the one that Anjali had planned with so much effort and gusto, Sid cancels just a week before the trip because he prioritizes an important meeting with Praveen about their biggest account. Anjali's anger meant that they did not talk for at least four months. Even after that, the cracks in the relationship just continue to grow. There were question marks with every decision being made.

As Sid's career graph is rising, his personal relationships continue to sputter and fail. But the euphoria of his rising career blinded him to everything else.

Creativity Unlimited was growing in stature every day. Sid was a darling of the media. He would be covered by magazines and TV channels almost every alternate month. Management institutes would call him to share his success story to inspire their students. Creativity Unlimited's new office was considered a showcase of what modern working offices should be like. They were also voted as one of the most aspirational places to work in India.

Everything was nice and shiny, but there were some shadows lurking in the dark.

The three-year retainer contract between Urjaa and Creativity Unlimited (which was finally signed), works out very well. Both companies grow by supporting each other. The turnover of Creativity Unlimited increases multifold as the share of digital advertisements by clients increases. Urjaa wins many new accounts and starts getting a share of the wallet from many of their existing accounts by using their secret weapon, Creativity Unlimited. It is a completely symbiotic, mutually beneficial relationship.

This seems to be a dream contract for Creativity Unlimited by any stretch of the imagination. Sid's approach is more people-oriented than money-oriented. He is focused more on his buddies than revenue. He does not hesitate to turn down a lucrative contract if he feels it makes his team stretched or unhappy. In his mind, the main strength of his company is its people and the unique way in which they are nurtured.

The success of the company is directly related to team morale, and this is to be protected at any cost. This was why he didn't jump at Urjaa's retainer contract. He takes it very slow, asking for a three-month pilot project between their companies. He makes sure both teams know each other and are comfortable before he signs the three-year retainer contract.

This contract brings immense stability to the finances of Creativity Unlimited. Sid can focus on improving the quality of their output rather than running after new clients. He spends more time training new buddies. He launches several new HR initiatives to make the buddies comfortable. He takes them for off-site meetings, keeping everyone happy and constantly motivated.

But on the flipside, Praveen's insistence on having Paul attend the meeting had the worst possible consequence for the autonomy with which Sid had been running the company. That meeting actually woke up a sleeping investor, who now wants to earn more money out of this company rather than just bragging rights. Praveen's parking lot chat with Paul sowed seeds of distrust about Sid's business sense in his mind.

Cracks start to appear in Sid's and Paul's relationship. Paul starts visiting Bangalore more often. He demands quarterly reviews and starts to monitor every lost opportunity. Paul is not really an expert in running a business, but he believes that continuously questioning Sid will keep him on track and maximize the business potential. Sid and Paul start to have arguments and disagreements on several issues. Sid may have been right in handling the business his way but as a majority shareholder, Paul would have his way.

Praveen, on the other hand, was sitting pretty and watching the fun. He didn't engage with Creativity Unlimited because he wanted to stay away from potential allegations of conflict of interest. The only reason he had engaged with them was because they had become a threat to the business; he had to sit up and take notice. He believed in the age-old saying—keep friends close and enemies closer.

When Sid had a meeting with Apex Computers, Mr Shroff called Praveen immediately. Praveen had excellent relationships with all his clients. He was their trusted confidant, so they would provide him with a lot of information, unrelated or not. Praveen took this call in a conference room in the presence of their CEO, who heard from the horse's mouth that Urjaa had strong competition. Praveen capitalized this and argued to the CEO that if they couldn't beat them, they should join them and manage them. Hence, he proposed a three-year retainer arrangement.

This isn't just a normal working arrangement—Praveen is watching how Sid and his team work very closely. He is using this to test the waters to see if he can somehow benefit more from Creativity Unlimited. For Praveen to benefit, he has to drive a wedge between Paul and Sid. That couldn't happen if Paul enjoyed his retired life in Kerala. So, he used his influence on Paul to drag him into the meeting.

Apart from their first private conversation in the parking lot, he followed up with several one-on-one conversations and emails with Paul. In fact, he would nudge Paul and drop hints about how he could manage Sid. Most of the arguments and fights Paul and Sid had, were a direct result of conversations between Paul and Praveen. Obviously, Sid is oblivious to Praveen's backseat driving strategy.

Paul, Praveen, and Sid were a nicely balanced equilateral triangle. All three of them were equidistant from each other and the sum of any two was greater than the third. This equilibrium, however, was under threat.

Today, Praveen has invited Paul and Sid for a dinner meeting supposedly to discuss the renewal of their contract six months later.

Paul and Sid reach The Lalit Ashok Hotel on Old Airport Road. Praveen is already seated in the restaurant. He extends a warm welcome. They exchange pleasantries. They order their drinks. Praveen is already sipping his single malt. Paul orders whiskey with soda and water. Sid sticks to orange juice. From his choice of drink, Praveen knows Sid's guard is up.

Praveen sets the ball rolling. "What do you think about our retainer contract, Sid?"

Sid says, "It is fantastic. The team is enjoying it. They look forward to every brief coming from the team. They do their best to satisfy your team. What is your perspective?"

Praveen says, "Oh, yes! My team is very happy with the output, too. They tell me that the clients are also very happy."

Sid says, "That is good to hear. I am sure it is working out well for your company. As I see you have won many new accounts in the last two years. I am sure our contribution has helped you with that. Interestingly, we were working with some of these clients through other advertising agencies like Orchid and we continue to work with them now that they are with you."

Praveen smiles and says, "Indeed! I thank you for your cooperation and support."

By now Paul is feeling left out so he tries to join the conversation.

Paul asks, "How has it worked out for you personally, Praveen sir?"

Before Praveen could respond, Sid says, "I think our engagement is a lucky charm for Praveen particularly. Within three months of signing the contract, he became the CEO. Ever since then, he has been the poster boy of the Indian advertising field. I see him more on TV than in the office."

They all laugh.

Praveen says, "That is true. Things have been good for the past couple of years. I don't know if it was because of the contract or not, but things changed since we signed the contract for sure. I can see Siddharth is not doing badly either. I read all his interviews in business magazines. You are really good, Siddharth."

"Thank you, Praveen!"

Sid is still not ready to call him sir.

Paul makes one more attempt to join the conversation.

Paul says, "You are the most successful CEO in India's advertising world. There are many other executives who aspire to be in your place, sir."

The only way Paul knew to impress people was by sucking up to them.

Praveen after a couple of drinks is slightly contemplative. He says, "Well, the grass is always greener on the other side. After spending so many years in the same company, everything becomes monotonous. There is no excitement. There is no freshness to the work like Siddharth and his team enjoy. Large companies tend to become very bureaucratic, so even in my position I feel like a cog in a giant wheel."

Paul says, "No, sir. You feel like 'cog-in-the-wheel'? That is impossible. "

But Sid knows Praveen is telling the truth. He listens carefully.

Praveen says, "No. This is for real. Yes, the money is good. There is stability. There is some limelight but still I think something is missing."

Sid says, "Maybe it is too stable. There is no excitement, no adventure."

"Exactly, Siddharth. That is what is missing."

Sid says, "Excitement and stability are opposite ends of the spectrum. You can't get both, I guess. And those who are used to stability may vie for excitement but may not be able to handle it."

Praveen says, "Well, it depends on life situation. I have worked for almost two and half decades to ensure I provide for my family. But soon my younger one will also step out for higher studies, and then I think even I will be ready for a little bit of adventure and excitement."

This takes Sid by surprise. But before he can react, Paul, in his third attempt to join the conversation, turns it decisively to business talk.

Paul says, "Our contract renewal is six months away. What did you want to discuss?"

Praveen pauses. He ponders over what he said in the last few minutes. He can't help but think that he opened up too much. He excuses himself for a restroom break. He comes back composed, and in his element again.

Praveen says, "I wanted to discuss the contract renewal terms with you."

Before Sid can respond, Paul quickly says, "I think we should increase the fees by 5–10%."

Paul's understanding doesn't go beyond fees.

Praveen nods but doesn't commit. Both of them now look at Sid.

Sid clears his throat and says, "The team will be happy if they get a bit of client exposure. If you could take us to your clients and help us understand what the client's needs are, we can contribute better."

Praveen asks, "Let me put it this way. Would you say you are happy about the contract clauses? Would you want to change anything?"

Praveen looks down at his glass to avoid eye contact with both of them. His tactic pays off. Both Paul and Sid speak simultaneously.

Sid says, "No."

Paul says, "Yes."

Both Paul and Sid are startled. This was the first time they had spoken against each other in public.

Sid is quick to make amends. He says, "I mean we want to work with you, and we are comfortable but of course,, we would like to increase our fees in line with the current market rates."

There is a moment of silence. Sid looks at Paul from the corner of his eye, doesn't respond, and just takes a sip from his glass.

Praveen asks, "Is that all?"

Sid knows very well that now he should keep quiet.

Paul asks, "Would Urjaa be open to changing any clause in the contract?"

In corporate negotiations, those who ask questions hold an upper hand over those who keep answering them.

Praveen smiles. He knows the conversation has taken a turn in the direction he wants. He says, "Everything is possible if you play your cards right."

Paul asks, "What do you mean?"

"I mean, you can keep the cake and eat it, too."

Paul asks, "You mean we can change the non-competing clause in the contract?"

"Kind of," Praveen says for the third time.

Inwardly, Paul is very excited but maintains a poker face.

"What cards do we have?"

"Everything. You are the best digital company in India. Your CEO is a poster boy for *Business Herald*. Anything is possible for you."

Paul asks, "But why are you opening your cards to us? What is in it for you?"

"I am interested in the growth of your company. I want it to grow multifold in the next five years."

"Thanks for your wishes, but I still don't get why you are so keen on it."

Paul knows what Praveen wants to say, but Paul wants to hear the words.

"Because personally, I am interested in your company."

It is music to Paul's ears. Sid starts to get uncomfortable.

Praveen continues, "Since I am the main negotiator on the other side, I will help you negotiate the contract term that is favorable to you in return for sweat equity, which I will hold in your company through my wife's company."

Praveen comes straight to the point. This is the corrupt and ugly face of Indian Corporate that Sid doesn't want to see. Paul maintains his calm and keeps asking questions.

"So you mean to say, you will help us remove the clause that we can't go to your clients directly?"

"Uh huh. That's right."

"So that's a huge growth potential for us."

"That's right. So I would like you to share a tiny part of the fortune with me."

Sid is a bit irritated. He doesn't like what he is hearing. He doesn't want Praveen to come so close to the company. So he says, "I am not sure if we can work directly with their clients."

"Why not?" Paul is surprised.

"We were testing the waters. I won't say we were successful. Besides, similar to what you did, other advertising agencies will come and stop us too, right?"

Sid has a point, but both of them don't want to accept this.

"That is not a big concern. At some point in time, you have to come out of the shadows," says Praveen.

"I agree," says Paul.

The precarious equilibrium among Praveen, Paul, and Sid crumbles. It becomes Paul and Praveen versus Sid.

Sid asks, "But why would you, as a CEO of Urjaa, agree to this? How does Urjaa benefit from the removal of the clause?"

Praveen smiles and says, "Leave that to me, Siddharth. Let me call for a champagne."

"Cheers," all of them say, but not in the same tone.

CHAPTER 5

Life Is Not Fair

Thrown into the deep end: sink or learn?

After that meeting, things start to look different for Sid. He now must watch his back. He knows something is brewing, but he cannot anticipate what it is. It doesn't look good. Sid is not against approaching large companies directly, but he doesn't like Praveen's approach. He doesn't like the corrupt foundation on which this strategy will likely be built.

Plus, he is definitely not comfortable having Praveen as a stakeholder in Creativity Unlimited. A well-wisher or a guide, sure, but his colluding with Paul is certainly not something he feels comfortable with.

Paul, on the other hand, doesn't see the operational difficulties in the strategy. He can neither anticipate nor understand that side of business. It is just the greed that sees this as an opportunity to make more money. Praveen's interest and active support in Creativity Unlimited make him believe he can multiply his wealth without doing much. Besides, whatever he has earned from Creativity Unlimited is because of Praveen anyway. He feels indebted to Praveen and feels compelled to listen to him.

Praveen is at an empty nest stage in life. He has successfully fulfilled his family obligations—sent both his children to good schools, provisions for their graduation and post-graduation, and kept a sum aside for them to start their lives. He has a comfortable home, a nice car, a club membership, and sufficient wealth to take care of himself and his family for the rest of their lives.

He now wants to create a legacy in the corporate world. His needs have reached the epitome of Maslow's hierarchy. He is already considered the most successful CEO in the advertising world, but he knows that conventional advertising is a sinking ship. Being known as a poster boy in the dying field is no way to leave the legacy behind. He now wants to jump on digital advertising—the future.

If he can make a mark in this field, then his legacy will last for decades, if not more. He has briefly considered starting his own company, but a couple of years of engagement with Creativity Unlimited opens his eyes to new ways of communication, the new media and the new mindset of young customers that he can't comprehend. He, therefore, decides to play his old association with Paul to his advantage and trade favors.

Internally in Urjaa, he plans to position this as a fait accompli. He plans to tell his board of directors that Creativity Unlimited refused to engage with them if the non-competition clause, which prohibits them from approaching Urjaa's customers, is removed. He plans to show a discount that is offered in lieu of this removal. Then he plans to guide Creativity Unlimited secretly to approach the clients and be successful. And when the time is right, he plans to jump the boat and be associated with Creativity Unlimited full-time in a suitable position.

With open disagreements between Paul and Sid, Praveen is using this opportunity to influence Paul directly. He has a series of secret meetings with Paul to chalk out how they can navigate the company into uncharted territory. It all boils down to who will lead this transition. Both of them can see that Sid is the biggest stumbling block in the transition. Convincing him is an option, but Paul rules it out. He knows Sid is stubborn and may not fully buy into this.

Paul also thinks Sid might try to close down the company if confronted. Paul has always been behind the scenes, so none of the employees know him well; for all of them, Sid is the leader and the whole company. For the plan to work, he needs to catch Sid off guard. So, Paul maintains a cordial working relationship with Sid but develops a secret plan with Praveen through their meetings.

Praveen sees this as a golden opportunity to fulfill his ambition. He knows Creativity Unlimited has a bright future. If done well, it can give all traditional ad agencies a run for their money. Or it can become an attractive option for traditional advertising agencies for strategic acquisition. He considers Creativity Unlimited as a gold mine, one that Sid is not willing to encash, and Paul is unaware of what its true worth is.

Over the last two decades of his experience in the corporate, he has learned an important lesson—wherever there is information asymmetry there is money to be made. He, therefore, plans to utilize this information asymmetry for his personal benefit.

After a series of meetings, Paul and Praveen decide to meet for one last time to finalizes the next steps. Paul invites Praveen to the Cosmopolitan Club in Jayanagar. This was once a happening place and the most sought-after destination for traditionally rich people of Bangalore, but now it appears to be caught in a time warp, looking quite old and dusty.

Paul has attended several meetings here with his bosses and holds this place in high regard. As soon as he could afford it, he takes a membership. He only brings important people here, when he feels that things are going to happen. Most waiters working there are from Kerala, so he inherently feels at home.

Praveen arrives at the club, the valet salutes him and asks for the key; Paul has arranged this to show his influence at this place. The doorman ushers Praveen to the room where Paul is sitting before him even saying why he is there. Paul is sitting there with a glass of whiskey in his hand. He greets Praveen with a firm handshake. Praveen holds Paul's hand firmly and turns it anticlockwise just a little bit to show he has an upper hand.

He orders, "Do you have a Single Malt? I would like one Glenfiddich on the rocks please."

The waiter nods and leaves. Paul is unfazed. This is an important discussion, and he needs Praveen to be in his comfort zone, especially with alcohol.

After the drink is served, Praveen takes the glass, swirls it a bit, smells the whiskey, and takes a sip.

Paul asks, "So, what do we do next?"

Praveen replies, "Let me recap on what we both agree. We both agree that Creativity Unlimited has a bright future if it starts directly dealing with the customers, rather than working with traditional ad agencies like Urjaa Advertising. But to do that we need someone who is experienced to head the business."

Paul agrees and says, "That is correct. We really need a specialist."

Praveen says, "Yes. We need someone who is really experienced in managing clients, who has a strong relationship with them, who knows how to make things work and get business."

Paul asks, "Do you have anyone in mind?"

Both of them know which way the conversation is headed. They both want the same end result but also want to maintain the upper hand. It is only a matter of time before someone blinks first.

Praveen says, "Yes, there are many who fit the description, but you need to ensure your company maintains the upward trajectory."

Paul says, "That is so true. That is precisely what I am worried about."

Praveen picks up his glass and takes a sip. The onus is now on Paul to broach the obvious.

Paul asks, "What is your plan with Urjaa? Have you encashed all your stock options? That's what I hear from the market."

Praveen is surprised. "You do have your ears to the ground."

Paul says with a smile, "My stock broker told me about the block deal. So you got your booty. What is left for you in Urjaa?"

Paul broaches the topic first but does it in a way that he still keeps the upper hand in the discussions.

Praveen says thoughtfully, "That is what I am thinking nowadays. What should I do next? What would be more challenging than Urjaa?"

Paul says, "Come join us. Creativity Unlimited needs you. I can offer you great stock options. Put you in the driving seat. Let us stretch our legs."

Praveen is happy that Paul has made this offer. That is what he wants. He is eager to take this up but wants to play it cool.

Praveen says, "It is not that easy. We still need to manage the clause in the contract."

Paul says, "Yes, that would be your precondition for joining us. Unless that clause is managed, it would be hard for us to accommodate you in our organization."

Praveen says, "It is not as easy as you think. I committed to it, but there will be hurdles."

Paul says, "I don't want to teach a fish how to swim. Experienced fish can swim well and not get caught in the net."

Praveen smiles. Paul raises the glass to say cheers, but Praveen isn't ready yet.

He asks, "But what about Sid? Will he fall in line? Otherwise, nothing will work."

Paul contemplates, "We have to go ahead with or without Sid. Leave it to me."

Now Praveen raises his glass and after the clink, both say, "Cheers!"

Sid, obviously, doesn't know about this meeting but he can notice the after-effects almost immediately. Paul starts to visit the office almost every day. He starts asking questions about every client, and every campaign. He starts to show his displeasure about revenues and also starts suggesting to Sid in no uncertain terms that they should pursue Praveen's strategy. Sid knows why Paul is behaving this way but doesn't know how to stop him.

Finally, one day he decides to confront Paul.

"Paul, can I talk to you about something important?" Sid asks.

Paul is waiting for this. He replies, "Oh sure. Let us go for lunch and talk peacefully." He doesn't wait for Sid to say yes, just starts walking toward the door.

Paul navigates his Toyota Innova through the notorious Bangalore traffic toward Indira Nagar. Paul has kept the volume of his car radio loud enough to discourage any discussion. Both are okay with this arrangement as they inwardly prepare for the imminent confrontation. As soon as his car arrives near the restaurant 'Little Italy', the guard removes the 'reserved' board from one of the parking lots outside the restaurant and salutes Paul.

Soon both of them are seated in a corner which has some privacy for them to discuss things.

"Has something changed off late? Are you not happy with the way the company is running?" Sid is as straightforward. That's the only way he knows how to deal with things.

Paul says, "We have done very well so far. Revenues are growing, profits are good, and employees are happy. I was so proud when I saw your picture all over the media. It was such a pleasant surprise!" It is hard to tell if Paul is genuinely happy or just being sarcastic.

"That was a surprise for me too. But what has changed? Why do I feel that I have no control?"

"What got us here will not take us further from here. We need to change our way of working. We need clients who will pay us what our efforts are truly worth."

It is hard to disagree with this so Sid nods along.

"So what do you suggest?"

"Follow Praveen's advice. Go for the kill."

"It is easier said than done, Mr Paul. Our organization is not ready for it."

"Why do you think so?"

"Because I know each and every one of them. I shaped them. They are young, brilliant, and creative but they are not mature, persuasive, and political. Those are essential qualities to deal with clients."

"Once you throw them in the deep end, they will learn to swim . . . "

" . . . or sink," Sid quips.

Paul gives him a stern look.

"They will have to learn."

"They can learn but it needs time."

"How much?"

"Two years, three maybe."

"We don't have that kind of time. The competition is springing up from everywhere."

"But we are ahead by at least three years. Before they can replicate our model, we will reinvent ourselves."

"Maybe we need help."

There is a long pause. There are no words, but Sid knows intuitively that Praveen is behind this thinking. He starts to get a sense of what their meetings might be about.

"In football, when a team wants to do better, they keep the captain but change the coach," says Paul.

Paul was trying to sound as non-threatening as possible. He was trying the 'with Sid' option first.

"A good coach can do miracles. He can help the captain achieve higher levels of performance," Paul says with a smile. He rarely smiles.

"The way I see it, Mr Paul, our business is more like cricket than soccer."

Paul has a question mark on his face.

"Here the captain has to play with the team to win. A coach can decide the strategy, but executing in the middle is easier said than done. A coach can't change the fortunes, only the captain can," says Sid. He speaks his mind as always, but little does he realize that he is digging his own grave.

He doesn't consider the possibility of him being replaced by someone else to take Creativity Unlimited forward. He mistakenly thinks that if he puts his foot down, Paul and Praveen won't be able to proceed on those lines. He is blissfully unaware of what is in store for him.

There is nothing much left to discuss. They eat their lunch without a word. They just pretend to attend to urgent things on their respective mobile phones.

Paul is not left with much of a choice. He has to choose between Sid and Praveen.

CHAPTER 6

Hard Reality

Life is stranger than fiction.

February 2016

Sid leans back and reads the email one more time.

It is quite clear that Paul has chosen Praveen over him. Sid thinks about Steve Jobs who was fired from Apple Inc., which was founded by him. Sid also realizes Steve Jobs was hired back. He is unsure of what to do next; he isn't Steve Jobs, and neither will he be hired back.

For the first time, he feels suffocated in the office. He decides to step out to get some fresh air. He walks aimlessly in Cubbon Park. There is a nip in the air. He walks faster. He reaches Vidhana Soudha, the iconic building housing state government offices. He walks up to the steps and sits there for a while watching the ongoing traffic.

He feels a little better. He is surprised that despite being in Bangalore for over a decade, he hasn't done this before. This is so close to the office, but he has never had the time to do this.

He realizes that it is impossible for him to hide this development from his buddies, especially Jo and Jee who can almost read his mind. He thinks of calling Anjali. It has been a while since he called her. Ever since the cancellation of the Ladakh bike trip, things have not been the same between them. Still, she is the only one he can talk to. He pulls out his mobile phone and calls her. She doesn't reply. He calls again. She cuts the line.

Sid says to himself, "I don't blame her. What else can she do? I seem to call her only when there is trouble."

He keeps watching the traffic mindlessly. After fifteen minutes, Anjali calls him back.

Anjali says, "Sid, why did you call at this time? It has never happened before. Is everything alright? Please tell me that you haven't met with an accident or something."

Sid says, "No, Anjali. I am fine. I am sitting on the steps of Vidhana Soudha, soaking up the sun."

Anjali says, "That is a great relief. I excused myself from the meeting since I was so worried. But wait a second, why are you sitting at Vidhana Soudha? Why are you not in the office?"

Sid says, "Paul and Praveen joined hands and sacked me." He chokes as he says this.

Anjali asks, "What? What do you mean they sacked you? This is your company. You are the CEO."

"Yes, that is correct but I am still a minority shareholder. Paul is the major shareholder and he also issued some shares reserved for the employee stock options to Praveen, so both of them together can technically do whatever they want."

There is a long pause on the other end of the phone line. Sid struggles to maintain composure.

"This is crazy, Sid. I still can't digest this news."

"Yeah. Me too. I am really lost."

Anjali says, "You hang in there. We will think of something. You don't give up. There may be some legal recourse. Let me check with my legal department."

Sid says, "No, Anjali. There is nothing we can do."

Anjali says, "Honey, I have to rush now. I stepped out of the meeting pretending to go to the restroom so I can't talk for long. But don't give up. I am with you. We will fight back."

Sid says, "Okay."

Anjali hangs up.

Sid starts to think that may be Anjali is right. He should fight for his turf. He should explore legal options. Afterall, he has built this company from scratch. How can he be unceremoniously evicted from it? But he is not sure. His sweat equity is untouched so Paul is not being too vindictive. He is lost.

So he instinctively decides to reach out to his guidebook in life Akbar-Birbal Stories. He flags an auto rickshaw, doesn't bother to haggle with the auto drivers, and heads home to refer to the Akbar and Birbal book.

He almost sprints upstairs to his room. The landlady is surprised to see him at this time but thinks to herself that his haste means that he must have forgotten something in his room. Sid flips through the book till he finds a story that he thinks could help.

Birbal and the List of Fools

Once Akbar summoned Birbal and asked him to make a list of five great fools in his kingdom. At first, Birbal thought it was a joke, but the Badshah was very serious. So Birbal set out to find the fools.

On his way, it started raining. So, he stopped under a tree. He saw a man nearby carrying a bucket of water and pouring it on his trees in the rain. Birbal asked him what he was doing. The man replied saying he needed his tree to grow faster, so he was watering it.

Birbal decided he had found his first fool.

Further on his journey, he met a man who was riding a mare but was carrying a bundle of grass on his head. Birbal asked him why he was doing so. The man replied, "My mare is pregnant, I don't wish to burden her with an extra load, so I am carrying the grass on my head instead." Birbal had found his second fool.

He then met a trader who looked very happy returning from a far-away country. Birbal asked him for the reason for his joy. The trader replied, "I had gone to another city for my business for a year and I made a lot of profit. But what makes me really happy is I got the news from my village that my wife is pregnant. I am over the moon that I am going to be a father. Birbal found his third fool.

He searched the rest of the kingdom but could not find anyone else he could call a fool. He returned to the court with three.

He narrated the stories of three great fools to Akbar in the court and all of them had a hearty laugh. Then Akbar asked, "Birbal, I had asked you to find five great fools, but you found only three. Where are the other two?"

Birbal calmly replied, "The fourth fool is me, Jahanpanah. Instead of using my capabilities to help the kingdom, I am busy finding fools." All the courtiers laugh the hardest at this.

Chuckling, Akbar asked, "What about the fifth and the greatest fool?"

Birbal said, "It is you, Jahanpanah. Instead of focusing on issues important to the kingdom, you are asking me to do these useless searches."

At this, Akbar got very angry. He banished Birbal from his kingdom.

Birbal knew that he had done nothing wrong, but he was punished because his point of view was not valued by Akbar anymore. So, he decided it was better to move away rather than fighting back or somehow trying to fit in. So Birbal moved away into oblivion, waiting for the right time to come back.

Sid closes the book and reflects on the story. Maybe Birbal is right. Maybe he should follow in Birbal's footsteps and step down rather than turn this into an ugly fight. If his opinion is also no longer valued, maybe this is his only recourse.

After spending an hour at home, he takes an auto back to the office.

Sid feels like he has seen this coming for the past six months, without realizing it. One can never really fully prepare oneself for such realities. It is like participating in fire drills in the office. Everything is smooth when you know it's just a fire drill, but when the actual fire breaks out, things are not so smooth and simple.

He feels angry, sad, and lost at the same time. He is angry at Paul's decision to throw him out in favor of Praveen, whom Sid considers an opportunist. He is sad that he has to leave this company and is completely lost because he hasn't really done anything else other than build this company since graduation.

So far, he has kept all his buddies out of this, they don't even have an inkling of what is going on behind the scenes. The only possibility he has speculated about is Praveen joining the organization and having to work with him. But leaving this company is not something he has envisioned, except perhaps in his worst nightmares. Now the worst nightmares have come true, and he has to deal with it.

It would have been better if Paul had a face-to-face discussion and communicated the decision to him, but instead Paul had chosen to send an email. "In a way, this is good too," Sid reasons with himself. "I will get more time to adjust to the new reality."

He calls for a town hall meeting with all the buddies.

The conference room is small and quickly becomes a crowded space with all the buddies scrambling in with their coffee. From the tone of communication, everyone knows this is no ordinary meeting. The speculation is ripe that the company is being taken over by a bigger company. Nobody is really prepared for what is coming their way.

"Dear buddies, as you all know, I founded this company about ten years ago in a one-bedroom apartment. Some of you have been with me since then. We have gone through many ups and downs. You have always stuck around. You have always believed in the company."

There is a pin-drop silence as Sid takes a pause. Nobody can still figure out which way this announcement is going.

"Unfortunately, companies are bigger than individuals. It has to be this way. Organizations carry on with or without people." Sid is speaking extempore.

"Over the last few weeks, I had several discussions with the board about how we can take our company, Creativity Unlimited, to greater heights, and how can we unleash its full potential. We all agreed that we are in the right place at the right time with the right team, but there were still some significant differences between the path forward."

There are light murmurs and some deep breaths as buddies realize what is coming their way. There is still hope that it is not as bad as they imagine.

"The board has decided to take a path that is undoubtedly the best; it's the path to growth and prosperity. However, somehow, I have realized that I am not the right person to take it forward."

There are sounds of displeasure around.

Sid raises his hand. Everyone quiets down and continues. "Ever since I started this company, my heart and brain were in unison. My heart told me what to do, my brain figured out how to do it. In the next journey, my heart is not with me. I may still be able to figure out how to take that path, but I don't want to do it without my heart.

"So, I have decided to step aside and let the board drive the company in the desired direction. They may find a suitable person to do it from outside the organization or from within."

The murmurs grow louder, sounding almost like protests. Some start tearing up, some are looking angrier with each passing sentence.

"I may wind up quickly and step aside, but I want you to do your best and work with the next leader as sincerely as you did with me. Just because I am stepping aside doesn't mean what they are doing is wrong. I want you all to promise you will do your best under a new leader and wholeheartedly cooperate with him or her. Can you all promise?"

"Promise!" It is a half-hearted reply from all the employees, with a lack of eye contact and more conversation between them.

"Do you promise?" Sid says a bit more loudly.

"Promise!" the response is now louder.

"Do you promise?" Sid almost shouts.

"Yes, we do promise!" the buddies match his tone reluctantly.

"Thank you, buddies, it was a pleasure working with you!" Sid says emotionally. His voice is hoarse, and he thinks a tear or two may roll down his face so he quickly goes back to his cabin. The buddies are aghast. They don't know what hit them.

Sid comes back to his cabin. For the very first time, he lowers all blinders to make his room into a private cabin. He sits at his table, wondering what to do next. He has only seen people being fired in movies and carrying their personal belongings in a cardboard box. The problem is Sid can't decide what is personal that he can take home and what belongs to the company.

He has several photographs of all their good moments, but they are with his buddies. He has many mementos and medals with his name on them but which he received only because of the company. He is too heartbroken and too angry to decide anything.

He just sits in the cabin without doing anything, hoping for some miracle to happen or something to show him the way. He prays that this was the right thing to do, and that deciding to follow a fictional character wasn't something he would regret.

There is a knock on the door. He wants no visitors, but he knows the knock is from people whom he cannot turn away. Without looking at the door, he says, "Yes, Jo, come in. Who else is with you?"

Jo and Jee make their way inside. Both of them are the first hires of Creativity Unlimited, who are close to Sid.

"Did they force you to resign?"

"No."

"Did they sack you?"

"No," Sid says, avoiding eye contact.

"Then why the hell are you going?" Jo asks.

"This is your goddamn company," says Jee.

"We are on your side. Stay here, we will fight with you," says Jo.

"No, guys. I am okay with the change. This is for the benefit of the company. This change is good for you."

Jo cannot hide her irritation. She says, "Sid, save this weird speech for people who don't know you enough. We know you. You nurtured this company, grew it out of nothing. How can you not be part of it when it is taking off?"

Jee says, "You are hiding something from us. You have to tell us everything."

Jo asks, "Who is behind this? Paul right? Who else?"

Jee asks, "What is changing? You said a change in direction. Are we becoming an ad agency?"

Sid says, "No, we are not. We will stay in the same business."

"Then is Paul selling us off? That gold-digging rascal. What is he up to?"

"Relax, guys. Nothing of that sort is happening. We will do the same business. We will be in the same office. You will do the same interesting work. Just the person in this cabin might be different."

"Who is it?" both of them ask in unison.

"Unfortunately, I don't know."

"You have to give us something."

Sid stays quiet. In his mind, he is searching for words. The trio is interrupted by a knock on the door. It's Julie, the office assistant, who walks in with an envelope addressed to Sid. Julie hands over the envelope but doesn't leave. She is interested in knowing what is changing, too. She is the only person who spends her entire day at the office, so a change of boss has the biggest impact on her. She wants to know sooner rather than later.

What can the envelope contain? Is it a legal notice for Sid? Is he being fired? All three of them think impatiently. Sid knows Paul will be pursuing direct business with the clients, but he is unable to figure out how Praveen fits into this arrangement. In the last few months, he has wondered many times about Praveen's role. He cannot figure out why Praveen is so keen on this development.

Maybe the envelope contains the answer, he thinks. Sid takes the envelope and tears it open. It is a new contract letter from Urjaa Advertising. It is sent at least a month before the previous contract expires. The mystery deepens.

"What the hell is happening? I don't understand this. Contract renewal is never so smooth," says Julie. She remembers the umpteen follow-up calls and emails she has to send to get the contract renewals. This is probably the first contract they have received before the due date. Sid is perplexed, too.

"Did you know about this?" Jo asks authoritatively.

"No, guys. I am as surprised as you are," confesses Sid.

"Let's read the contract and see if there are any clues," says Julie.

Although Sid doesn't know for sure, he can guess that the non-competitors clause must have changed.

"Go to the non-competition clause, Julie."

The non-competition clause has completely changed. It now reads.

Considering the evolving market situation, Urjaa wishes to end the exclusivity clause in the previous contract on either side. Urjaa reserves its rights to work with other digital agencies while recognizing that Creativity Unlimited may be free to work with clients of Urjaa directly, without involving them.

Sometimes, while walking in a pitch-dark forest, unable to figure out where you are and which way you are going, there can be a flash of lightning that illuminates the world around you, giving you a crystal-clear picture. The renewal letter had the same effect. Suddenly, Sid has no more questions and knows exactly who the next occupant of his cabin is. But he doesn't have the heart to share it with Jo, Jee, and Julie.

In the meantime, far away from the office, in the Cosmopolitan Club in Jayanagar, Praveen and Paul get together again. It is going exactly as per their agreement a few weeks ago. Paul conducts a series of meetings with Sid to get him on board to go beyond advertising agencies. But he stands his ground. He insists they would fail if they jumped right into it. He asks for the years to be ready. Paul and Praveen don't have that time. It is a stalemate situation.

The only option is to let him go. Paul likes Sid but now his utility is over. Sid has to go. But Paul won't do it unless he has assurance on two things. One, that Urjaa releases them from the binding non-competing clause, and two, that Praveen joins them to steer the ship. They meet in the club to share the drafts of agreements and the letter to Sid with each other.

Both of them operate shrewdly, taking one confidence-building measure at a time. It pays off. Praveen couriers the renewal letter and Paul sends the email to Sid exactly at the same time.

Sid leaves, and the contract is received. Paul and Praveen are together to celebrate.

"Cheers," both say with beaming smiles.

"Now begins stage three of our plan," says Paul. "We have to get you onboard."

"That's true. I am ready to take the plunge. But there are some loose ends to be tied."

"Loose ends like what?" Paul asks, surprised.

"I need to secure my future. I need time to lie low for a while before joining you."

"Really? You never mentioned that." Paul hates surprises.

"Yes, I didn't. If I did, you wouldn't have hastened Sid's exit."

Paul has half a mind to cancel the whole deal. Praveen should not have hidden this from him. But Paul now realizes that he is on the receiving end as he is handing over the reins to Praveen, so he is forced to give him the time and space he needs.

"How long do you need."

"Six months," Praveen says nonchalantly.

"Why?"

"My exit clause says that if I join any competitor or a company in a similar field, otherwise they can take legal action on me. I can't afford to burn the bridge. "

"So what do we do for six months?" Paul is trying his best not to sound desperate.

"Think about it. Sid started this company. He has handpicked every single person. If he exists and I join the next day, all of them will hate me. They will blame me for his exit."

"So what do you suggest?"

"We need to give it six months."

"Six months? Who leads the company till then?"

"You will have to do it."

"Me? They hardly know me. How will that work?"

Paul can feel cold sweat emerging from his head and flowing down behind his ear. He hasn't seen this coming. The balance of power has changed. Now Praveen is calling the shots. Paul has no choice.

"Don't worry. You are not alone. I will work with you all the time. We can meet every day. This transition is necessary for our success. If I join straight away, I am quite sure the team will not cooperate with me."

Paul can't argue. He feels helpless and starts doubting his plan for the first time.

The next few months are hell for Paul. He struggles to manage his own company. He has daily confrontations with his employees, who see him as a villain who got rid of their beloved Sid. Several projects fail, clients become unhappy, and they threaten to terminate their contracts. There is a question mark on everything in Creativity Unlimited.

The stage is set for Praveen to take charge and dazzle.

CHAPTER 7

Life Is Not Easy

Finding common ground can sometimes
lead to double the unhappiness.

The buddies had the most annoying eight months. The time that they worked with Sid at Creativity Unlimited was the most enjoyable part of their lives. It did not compare to college, and sometimes not even to their vacations, how much fun ten years at Creativity Unlimited had been.

But things had taken an abrupt U-turn in the last eight months. Since that fateful day when Sid told them about his decision to move on, everything went downhill. Sid's youthful, warm, and lively presence in the office was replaced by the dull and uninspiring presence of Paul. Before Paul, they could sit anywhere, bring their bean bags to work, and even their music systems. All that went out of the window, quite literally.

They turn up in the office on a Monday and suddenly find themselves surrounded by structured cubicles and blue and dull gray walls. The change is shocking and abrupt, resulting in some turning home and reporting sick. Unfortunately, it was just the beginning of the crazy changes coming their way. Paul scraps the famous 'anytime work-time' policy, asking everyone to report at 9 o'clock sharp.

Jo asks Paul, "9 o'clock is fine, but are you referring to a.m. or p.m.?" She had no idea why some of her buddies laughed. They start attending status meetings, which they could not make sense of. Unlimited leaves were replaced with 15 days of casual leaves and 14 days of sick leave. They can no longer announce that they are on leave but have to fill up some form and attach the required documents.

In short, Creativity Unlimited is turned into any other limited company. In a matter of eight months, Paul takes the most fun company to work in and turns it into the most boring snooze fest anyone has ever seen. Some buddies who think practically decide to move on. They argue that if Creativity Unlimited is going to lose its uniqueness then what is the point in sticking around; it is better to find the company that pays them higher salary. Others, who consider themselves eternal optimist, stick around hoping that someone will come and rescue them from the great expanse of monotony created by Paul.

Today is the day their new boss arrives. In their opinion, any living being would be a better boss than Paul. A handful of them know Praveen, but most of them don't. There is gossip going around on whether the boss actually would be him and how he would be as a boss. Because of the incessant disciplining by Paul and the special circular which he sent to everyone; most employees are in the office at 9 a.m. sharp. Paul has asked Praveen to reach 9:30 a.m. to start his first day at the office.

Secretly, in his heart of hearts, Paul is also eagerly waiting for Praveen to come and take over the reins. He has also hated working for the last eight months. He never came to the office on time but had a habit of randomly calling some employees to check on who is in the office and who is not. All this policing and disciplining put pressure on him, too.

When Sid was in charge, he was free. He could stay in Bangalore or Kerala or go on vacation, it didn't matter. Sid took care of everything. In short, all the souls in the office of Creativity Unlimited are eagerly awaiting to be rescued by Praveen.

Praveen makes an energetic entry into the office. To look young, he has significantly changed his looks. He has cropped his hair thin; he is wearing trendy glasses, blue jeans, and a printed T-shirt.

He says in an enthusiastic voice, "Hi, buddies, how are you today?"

He is expecting smiles and informal replies, but instead, the group listlessly starts applauding as instructed by Paul. Praveen is surprised by this traditional welcome and can also sense the group's reluctance in the claps.

When the applause dies down, Paul clears his throat and starts speaking, "Dear Employees . . . "

Paul has this uncanny knack of pissing people off within the first few seconds. He lives up to his reputation even on this day. He still doesn't call them 'buddies' as what they prefer and presses on with his speech.

"Dear Employees, I am pleased to announce the appointment of Mr Praveen Kumar as the Managing Director of Creativity Unlimited with effect from today. He has an illustrious career of twenty-five years in advertising, media, and communication."

Paul has learned the speech by heart but today, he forgets. So he fumbles and reaches for his notes in his pockets. Tries to read but he can't without his reading glasses. So he holds the notes in his mouth and fumbles one more time to get his reading glasses out. Then, he starts reading again right from the top.

"Dear Employees, I am pleased to announce the appointment of Mr Praveen Kumar as the Managing Director of Creativity Unlimited with effect from today. He has an illustrious career of twenty-five years in advertising, media, and communication. He has been associated with Creativity Unlimited in the capacity of a client for the last six years and has guided us through the complex changes in the industry.

"We have changed, the situation around us has changed, so we can no longer do the same things we did in the past to achieve our goals. So as the chairman of this company, I decided to make a change and here we are."

Paul takes a pause and looks at everyone. He is met with cold stares. He is now at the last sentence; if this goes off well, then he can escape this ordeal forever, he thinks. Since the last sentence is simple, he doesn't have to refer to the notes again, he says, "I now invite our dear friend Sid to address all of us."

There are gasps and giggles. What an epic faux pas by Paul. Evidently, Paul has not been able to get Sid out of his mind either. Praveen's face turns red. This is not the start he has hoped for. Paul needs a resurrection act quickly. He acts as if he has made a deliberate joke and starts laughing aloud with a 'gotcha' facial expression. Uncertain laughter can be heard in the crowd. Then in a more formal tone, he says, "I invite Praveen to address us."

There is mild applause. All eyes are on Praveen now.

Praveen shakes off the mistake and faces the crowd. "Thanks, Paul. This is excellent. I am very excited to be here. We are at the cusp of big growth. Bright days await us at the next turn. All we need to do is dare to walk the path. I promise all of you will be richer in a few years from now if you support me. What we have achieved so far is great but it's not enough. What got us here will not take us further.

"The path ahead is different, so the strategy ahead has to be different. I hope you will walk this path with me because one thing I am sure about is, I can't do this alone. I need everyone's support. We all need to be on top of our game and I'm sure we will win. Thanks again, Paul."

Scattered applause meets his speech, but Paul claps the loudest. He is impressed that Praveen delivered such an eloquent speech without referring to any paper. It is a good come back from the mess he created a while ago. The assembly is dismissed. Paul has arranged a South Indian breakfast for everyone. But nobody is interested. Paul and Praveen go to the cabin. Thambi fills a few plates with all the available delicacies and brings two cups of filter coffee to the room.

Buddies disperse with murmurs, with mostly sarcastic takes on Praveen's speech.

"Who wants to be prosperous, I left my father's house where I was prosperous. It stinks."

"We are here to have fun; what about that?"

"He said we have to be on top of the game . . . which game was he referring to? Nintendo?"

"Who eats this idly-dosa shit for breakfast? Does he know us or what?"

The consensus is Praveen and Paul are from Mars, and the buddies and Sid are from Venus. Somehow, both have to manage themselves on the Earth.

***

Praveen is keen to show his impact straightaway. He wants to win a new client as early as possible. He has already decided that his best chance is with LTR, a traditional South Indian food giant with a hundred years of history. The owners are simple and humble; they swear by the legacy and secrecy of their recipes. They hold Praveen in very high regard.

Praveen has worked painstakingly for years to build trust and win them over. They are obviously the first choice to win over from Urjaa to Creativity Unlimited. He thinks it's a slam dunk case.

Praveen has to choose a couple of bright buddies, take them to LTR, get introduced, and get started. He calls Jo and Jee, the most creative minds, to go with him. He calls them to his cabin for a briefing.

Jo is wearing her usual spaghetti strap top and short skirt with colorful flip-flops. She has a tattoo of a butterfly on her left shoulder. Jee is wearing a dull gray T-shirt with bold block letters, which can neither be read nor mean anything. He is wearing distressed jeans, chewing a gum, and has a condescending look on his face. Praveen looks at them and knows that they need to change their look first before they can even hope to get anything from LTR. But he doesn't want to start on the wrong foot. So he starts talking about the account.

"You must have heard about LTR, right?"

Jee says, "Ya ya, back home my mum used to make all this dosa-idli stuff with that. Same shit right?"

"Yes, same dosa-idli guys but no shit." Praveen tries to crack a joke but Jo and Jee are unimpressed.

"What about them?" Jo asks.

"They did huge countrywide research to understand their customers. They found that their products are very popular among 40+ customers. . ."

"You mean uncles and aunties . . . " Jo has a bad habit of interrupting; it doesn't matter who she is talking to.

"Yes, correct. And they found that young customers below 25 hate their products."

"Why do they need countrywide research to find this out?" Jee says, making an intelligent point with his customary rude tone.

"Not a single soul out there likes LTR," he continues, pointing at the buddies.

Praveen is not used to this. In Urjaa, when he spoke, everyone listened. Nobody dared to cut him off or talk to him like these guys were. Here, a couple of youngsters, half his age, are challenging him. Clearly, this place is not easy to navigate.

"Don't tell me he wants to hire us to sell his products to blokes like us." It is Jo, one step ahead in the conversation. Both laugh and give each other a high-five commiserating their lack of interest in the brand.

"As a matter of fact, they do," Praveen says. "They want to hire us so we can help them to market their products to young customers."

"But that is impossible; everyone hates their products, their logo, even their color schemes."

Praveen is running thin on patience.

"Don't worry, I have handled many such projects where they thought it is impossible to change perceptions of customers but through cleverly crafted campaigns, I did."

Jo and Jee exchange a look.

"I have everything worked out. We should just go to meet Ramaiah next Monday. I will have everything planned. You will just support me in the meeting."

Jee tries to argue. "Listen, Pee . . . " He accidentally blurts out Praveen's nickname among the buddies. "I hope you don't mind us calling you P. It's not going to happen unless they change something big. Who gives a shit about tradition these days? Nobody is impressed with a century-old recipe . . . They need to change."

Praveen clears his throat and says, "Well, their survey also revealed that the younger generation preferred their products in a blind test. So, they believe that youngsters will buy their product if communicated correctly."

"No, dude, it doesn't work that way," Jo tries to pitch in.

Praveen has two new names in the last minute and he is being drawn into an argument, which he is definitely not used to.

"Guys, listen up. I said I have everything worked out," he says, lifting his index finger, "all you need to do is accompany me there and participate in the conversations with me."

Jo and Jee nod. They don't like the index finger being pointed at them.

It brings to mind the language they hear at home and the reasons behind their decision to move out. They wish to get out of the cabin. Praveen adds, "Listen, fellas," as they open the door to go. "There's one more thing. You cannot come to the meeting in this manner. You must dress appropriately. Don't flaunt your belly ring or tattoo.

Jo and Jee are terribly agitated. They wonder if it is Praveen or their parents talking to them. Praveen, though, goes on and on.

"Jee, please shave before you come and, Jo, do something with your hair."

It is obvious that there is mutual contempt.

Both Jo and Jee go for a cigarette and spend the rest of the afternoon brooding.

This is clearly not going to be simple for anyone.

CHAPTER 8

When Rubber Hits
the Road . . .

Navigating the twists of corporate dynamics.

Praveen's car—a BMW 3-series—approaches the LTR office. The guard salutes and opens the gate. Only a few selected VIPs like Praveen are allowed to park inside the office. Praveen is dressed in a white full sleeves shirt and gray trousers, colors preferred by the LTR owner, Ramaiah. He checks all the parked cars to figure out if Ramaiah and his brothers have reached the office. As always, they have.

In his broken Kannada, he asks the security guard, "*Channa gidiya? Tiffin aayata?*"

This is the most popular way of checking the welfare in Bangalore—the status of the last meal. If they have had the last meal, then everything is considered alright.

"Has my team reached the office?" he asks the person sitting there with the register.

"No, sir, but two kids were trying to enter our office by taking your name. I made them sit outside."

Praveen smiles. How would the guard know that he has changed his job, he thinks.

"Where are they?" he asks.

"Sitting there. But they can't be your colleagues. They look strange."

Now Praveen is worried. He walks across to Jo and Jee. He is shocked by what he sees. He remembers asking Jo to do something with her hair, but he didn't mean to color them green. He is aghast to see a girl with green hair, a sleeveless top, and a short skirt. There is nothing he can say or do.

Jee has shaved as told, combed and gelled his hair, but he has a new earring, which Praveen is sure was not there before. Jee looks very uncomfortable in a long-sleeve shirt, and is still wearing torn jeans.

"Why are you still wearing torn jeans?" Praveen says angrily.

"It wasn't torn when I left the house," Jee says straight-faced.

Jo chuckles. They still can't understand how their clothing and appearance connect to winning the account. They also wonder if Praveen had everything worked out, why he is worried about what they are wearing?

Without any other choice, Praveen brings them into Mr Ramaiah's office. It is the same office his father had used and perhaps his grandfather, too. They see a large wooden desk with a glass top and a few artifacts as they enter. There are five heavy wooden chairs in front. On their right are Ganesh and Tirupati idols with garlands and *agarbatti* still puffing out a last bit of smoke.

On their left, there are mementos and awards LTR has received. Right in the center is a painting of a man from the previous century who was the founder of LTR. The cabin has a lingering scent of jasmine. Ramaiah's office is clearly stuck in a time warp as the rest of the world has moved ahead.

Soon, Mr Ramaiah walks in. Wearing a dhoti and a long-sleeved shirt, he is dressed entirely in white. He also has oil in his hair and is wearing thick-framed glasses. He extends a warm smile to Praveen and folds his palms to welcome everyone else. That falters the minute he sees Jo. He has probably never seen anyone with green hair and he is wondering why someone would do that.

The best he can do is to ignore her and try to talk to Praveen. Jo and Jee are wondering what they are doing there and have a strong urge to look at their phones. They have been warned by Praveen not to touch their phones in front of Ramaiah.

Ramaiah seemed settled with a strange group of people sitting in front of him; Praveen whom he knew very closely, and the other two who seemed to be aliens.

"So are you settled in the new job? I am sure it is not easy."

"It is not too difficult either. I have worked with Creativity Unlimited for a long time already. I knew most of the people."

Soon, filter coffee is served in traditional steel cups. Praveen turns to Jo and Jee and says, "This is the best coffee in the world. This is a special brew prepared by Ramaiah's grandfather and is served only at this office. It is amazing."

Praveen kills two birds with one stone. He flaunts his proximity to Mr Ramaiah to his colleagues and manages to impress Ramaiah himself.

Jo and Jee don't care. Ramaiah is impressed.

They keep discussing little things over coffee. Once done, they start discussing business.

Ramaiah clears his throat, "We are concerned about our company's future. Since a lot is changing, we are unsure if our company will endure. While the younger generations, like your coworkers, don't think highly of us, all the older generations do. We are baffled as to why. For the previous four to five generations, our items were in high demand, so we didn't have to worry about our popularity with the next generation. However, times have changed since then. "We can't understand the next generation. It's almost as if they are aliens." Ramaiah glances involuntarily at Jo as he says the last line.

This is when Praveen realizes that he hasn't introduced his colleagues.

"This is Jyotichandrika, our creative artist. We call her Jyoti."

Jee tries his best to keep a straight face; Jo tries to remember the last time anyone called her that. Ramaiah could have never guessed in his wildest dreams that the person with green hair would have a name that sounded like his grandmother's.

"And this is Jeetendraprasad, our media specialist. We call him Jeetu."

Praveen does not want to call them Jo and Jee—this would sound ridiculous to Ramaiah.

Ramaiah folds his hands to greet them, but they don't know how to respond. So, they just smile in return.

Praveen continues, "We understand your concern and we think it is right for you to worry. We have seen many other companies losing their business because they could not make themselves relevant to the new generation. One of the major mistakes they made was relying on traditional media to reach out to young customers. That is never going to work."

Praveen takes a pause and looks at everyone. Ramaiah is leaning forward in his chair and listening intently. Jo and Jee are trying to look at Ramaiah but still avoiding direct contact.

"I realized this when I was working in Urjaa. I tried to convince the management but they have high stakes in conventional media, so they are behaving like ostriches with their heads buried in the sand, refusing to acknowledge the incoming onslaught of the new digital media. This is why I decided to move on to Creativity Unlimited. Here, we focus on communicating to the younger generation in a language they understand, in a medium they watch. I am confident we will be able to popularize your brand among the young generation."

Ramaiah has questions. "But how do you communicate with them when they don't watch any TV or read any newsletter?"

Praveen says, "They don't watch TV, but they watch YouTube. They don't read newspapers, but they read blogs. They don't look at hoardings, but they are always on Facebook, Twitter, and Instagram. So, we market your messages on these mediums."

Praveen and Ramaiah were hitting it off, but Jo and Jee were growing restless. Praveen was right in saying what he said but that wasn't everything they did. They did that and a lot more.

Ramaiah asks, "But how do you do that?"

Praveen now looks at Jo who is the creative head. She is reluctant to speak but everyone is looking at her and expecting her to say something.

Jo says, "Before we decide to come up with creatives, we need to see the product from the eyes of people like us. We need to understand what they like and what they don't. Then we create JPEGs, GIFs, .mov files which Jee puts into the right places."

Ramaiah has no clue what JPEGs and GIFs mean but it sounds very snazzy and different, so he is happy.

"We have recently completed in-depth research on this. We will let you use it. Our agency has done a great job in understanding them." He signals to his assistant who comes in with a few spiral bound booklets and hands them over to Praveen and his team. Out of curiosity, Jo and Jee start flipping through them. The booklets are full of PowerPoint presentations, graphs, charts and analysis which the agency has done. After flipping through a few pages, they immediately lose interest.

Praveen says, "This is wonderful. It will definitely come in handy."

Jee says, "This is great, no doubt, but not enough. This won't inspire Jo to come up with the campaign. Usually, we don't rely on this kind of research. We do our own observations before we create the campaign."

Ramaiah doesn't look pleased with this comment. Praveen senses that.

"Do you mean the in-depth analysis we have done, the crores of rupees we have spent, is not useful to you and you want to do something else?" Ramaiah says, almost angrily.

Jee says with the same condescending look that he always has, "Well, I can't comment on that but all I can say is this may not be useful for us."

Jo nods. Ramaiah doesn't want to talk to both of them, so he looks at Praveen.

"Praveen, this is exactly what we used to give you when you were in Urjaa. You gave us so many great campaigns. So won't it work this time too?"

"Of course, it will. I will work with the team personally to deliver the campaigns to you. Can you please ask someone to keep these reports in my car?"

Praveen needs a distraction to cool things down.

Jo tries to say something but Praveen signals to her to keep quiet.

Praveen tries to wrap things up. "We will take about 15 days to go through the reports and come up with a campaign."

"Sure." Ramaiah is already tapping his right hand on the desk signaling the end of the meeting.

"When can you give us the contract? That is required for us to start working on this campaign immediately."

Ramaiah's face turns stern.

"Well, the contract was ready, and I was about to hand it over, but I think I need to put one more condition in the contract."

"And what would that be?"

"I would like to evaluate this agency on the success of this campaign. If this campaign is successful, we will continue. Otherwise, we may want to go back to Urjaa."

Praveen is shaken. He hasn't seen this coming. He thought a fifteen-year relationship with LTR would be enough to pull this contract off. But it isn't. He still has to jump through some hoops before he lands a long-term relationship with LTR again.

This is certainly beyond the script, and he hopes it's the first and last experience he has that goes this way.

CHAPTER 9

Divergence

Confronting challenges and seeking alternate routes.

Back in Praveen's office, Jo and Jee are sitting with the pile of spiral-bound research reports, trying to make sense of insights from the report. Praveen is trying to find out whether they are well-equipped to interpret the report and develop the campaign. Both Jo and Jee are bright, so they convince Praveen that they can do it, but they still think it's not a particularly useful activity. So, their heart is not in it.

Suddenly, Praveen's phone rings. It is Paul. He is calling to ask Praveen to join him for a coffee at The Lalit Ashok Hotel at Old Airport road. He wants to know how the meeting went but doesn't want to come to the office. Praveen leaves hurriedly. Jo and Jee are by themselves in the room.

Jee closes the thick report as soon as Praveen leaves the room.

"Dude, I think we are screwed. I don't think this P-guy and that Ram-guy get it."

"Obviously, they don't, and they won't." Jo is known to be judgmental.

"Basically, they aren't accepting that they are doing it all wrong."

"Who is going to eat their *laddoos* and *murukku* man?"

"Yeah! It was all okay till we didn't have burgers and pizzas."

"Now I hardly know anyone who doesn't like pizza or pasta. Who eats these laddoos and *patra vadi* and all."

"Hey, listen, the other day that Vee-dude told his girlfriend 'You can't make everyone happy, you are not pizza.'"

Both of them chuckle. This silly joke is a good relief to rising tempers.

Jo says, "I don't know about you but one of the reasons I looked for a job outside my city was because I wanted to enjoy the food I liked, anytime, every time. All my mum used to make was this LTR all the time."

"Same here, dude. Exactly the same."

"So, what are we going to do? I can understand what is written in the reports."

"Really? What a relief." Jee mimics Praveen and both of them laugh.

" . . . but I don't agree with one word. I think all the blokes who were interviewed were either old or they were lying. None of this makes sense."

"I agree. There is nothing in this report that we can actually use for either designing the campaign or the media coverage for it."

"I wish we had Sid with us now. He would have told Ram-dude on this face that these reports are crap."

"Yeah, man! I miss him too."

"He never taught us to lie or hide our opinions, so I don't know what to do now."

"Pee-dude wants us to come up with an analysis and a campaign but we are not convinced. So we stand our ground. We tell him we are not convinced."

"Done deal!"

"*Chal.* Let's go for a *sutta.*"

Praveen drives his bimmer to The Lalit Ashok. It's a grand pink structure that reminds him of palaces in Rajasthan. He alights and allows the valet to take over the car. For all such meetings, Praveen drives the car himself. He argues, "BMW is the ultimate driving machine . . . why should I allow my driver to have all the fun?" But the real reason is that he wants to keep such meetings a secret. He harbors trust issues with everyone around him.

He makes his way to the coffee shop where Paul is waiting for him.

After exchanging pleasantries, Paul asks, "How did the meeting go?"

"Fantastic. LTR is on board. They are ready to work with us. They already gave us the first assignment."

"Really? That's great news!" Paul says this but he can sense that something is amiss.

"But we need to educate our team to deal with clients like LTR. That Jyotichandrika colored her hair green. Imagine."

"Who is Jyotichandrika?" Paul hasn't figured out the real names in the eight months he spent disciplining them.

"That creative head girl, Jo."

"Oh ya. Jo. Something is wrong with her. When I took over from Sid, she shaved her head as a mark of protest. Imagine a bald young girl, such an ugly sight."

Praveen doesn't know what to say but he was thankful that Jo colored her hair rather than becoming bald. If Ramaiah had seen a bald girl, he would have been too shocked to continue with the meeting.

"Maybe you should take out a circular banning them from coming to the office like this." Paul clearly belonged to a different world.

"Circular may not work. I will handle it."

"So did they sign a contract for three or five years?"

"We are first timers right, they will sign for three years."

"They will sign? Haven't they already done it?"

"Technically they have confirmed but the document isn't with me."

"Why?"

"They want to add an exit clause after the first three months. If they don't like our first campaign, they want to exit," Praveen says, his worry apparent.

"Oh no! That doesn't sound good. What happened? Why did they back out?"

"Technically they didn't back out. The contract wasn't signed yet, so they are free to change the terms."

"Praveen, you know what I mean right? This is not what we hoped or planned for."

"Yes, I know. I was hoping to use my personal equations to win the first contract and then leverage this contract to win other customers before the word spreads in the ad agencies that we are bypassing them to go to end customers directly."

"Yeah, that is what you told me. Now, what do we do?"

"I need a plan B. We can't go to other customers till we have LTR on board for three years. We can't let the word spread. We have to continue working with the ad agencies as usual till we have LTR in our kitty."

"Do you think that will work?"

"It has to work. We don't have any choice. If the word gets out that we are going to companies directly, all ad agencies will terminate their contracts and we will be in no man's land."

"That doesn't sound good. Do whatever it takes to avert this."

"I know. Will not let that happen."

"You better not let that happen. I have too much at stake."

"Me too."

The meeting ends at 4:30 p.m. Praveen decides to go home instead of office to avoid the traffic that builds up in Bangalore after office hours.

CHAPTER 10

What Got You Here . . .

A quest for brand rejuvenation.

Praveen has his task cut out for him. He needs to put up a credible campaign, launch it, and show some results so he can walk away with a three-year contract. He knows this may not be as simple as it sounds. He has to work with two unruly colored-hair, tattooed, belly-ringed creative people with a mind of their own.

He decides to brief them about the brand and its heritage for them to come up with a creative campaign. LTR's brand identity was entirely his creation. He took LTR from a local brand, which was famous only in some parts of Bangalore to all of India. He built it brick by brick, product by product, package by package, and store by store. He is very proud of his achievement. He thinks he knows more about the LTR brand than Ramaiah himself.

But now he is at a crossroads. The strong traditional position he had taken a few years ago doesn't augur well with the new generation. They despise the brand. So, he has to change the positioning, or packaging . . . or product . . . or SOMETHING that would make the brand relevant to them.

He tries hard to explain the positioning of the brand. He shows them the research, which rates the brand very highly, but no avail. Both Jo and Jee are expressionless. They have made up their mind that it's not going to work. Irritated, Praveen decides to pull his rank on them. He orders them to redesign the packaging and develop a different logo design with a youthful tagline.

Jo and Jee are shocked by this assertion. They haven't imagined working under pressure. They don't know how to do it.

Jo says, "I didn't see that coming."

"Neither did I."

"He should have at least listened to our idea."

"Ya, man! I think it will work, but this guy doesn't agree."

"What are we gonna do?"

"Chal sutta maarte hai. Dekh lenge."

For Jo, Jee, and many others like them, solutions to any problem could be found in a cigarette, and anything could be celebrated with a beer.

Praveen has several meetings with them to finalize things, but these are neither constructive nor conclusive.

"Why did you change brand colors in this packaging design?" Praveen almost yells.

"You told me to create something youthful. The brand colors are most un-youthful!"

"But they are the assets of the brand. They are designed with some clear thought in mind."

"Yes, but it's exactly this thought that is stopping us from targeting the youth."

"I don't care, don't change the brand color."

"Okay, boss. Let me see what I can do." Jee's sarcasm drips in his use of the word 'boss' for the first time in the office.

"What? In this ad storyboard, you are showing the mom wearing a skirt and blouse and not traditional wear?"

"Yeah, of course. Dudes of my generation want to see their moms like this, not in the traditional wear," argues Jee.

"But this completely uproots the foundation of the brand."

"Pee-dude, we can't reposition unless we change something." Jee isn't afraid to make his point known.

Praveen hated being called Pee-dude. He tries to get over his irritation and calm himself down.

"Look here, Jeetendraprasad, we have to build the brand on the assets we have. We have to preserve the position and build something that's suitable for the new generation. It is like you have a room in your parental home that needs to be renovated to make it youthful. Not demolish the house to build your room."

Jee hates being called by his full name, so they are even now.

"You want to hear the truth? We hate such rooms. You can never reposition a brand by giving young people just a room. You need to think from scratch. Not necessarily destroy what you have, but carry out significant change."

"It doesn't work that way. You don't have enough experience in managing brands." Praveen runs out of arguments and decides to pull rank, his favorite weapon.

"Listen, Pee-dude, you are missing a big point. I am the target customer for this campaign, too. You are trying to find me as a customer, too. So as a customer, I am telling you, these minor tweaks won't work."

Jee storms out of Praveen's cabin.

Jo escapes, Jee confronts. The result is the same. Praveen's ideas are not going anywhere. The clock is ticking. Praveen has a tough time showing a brave face to both Paul and Ramaiah. Despite multiple assurances from Praveen, they remain cautious about what they are likely to see. Praveen keeps pushing and prodding his team Jo and Jee to come up with something that he can show to Ramaiah.

Days and weeks pass by as D-day approaches. Praveen is growing very nervous as his reputation, and personal credibility are all at stake.

Will he be able to impress Ramaiah all over again?

Praveen pulls up his car in front of LTR's office. The security guard salutes, removes the 'reserved' sign, and allows Praveen to park his car. Jee and Jo are also with him. Praveen doesn't want to take any chances with their coming late or dressing weirdly. He has ensured they wear clothes suitable for the meeting and turn up on time.

The security guard waits for a familiar smile and some general questions in broken Kannada that Praveen usually asks. Praveen ignores him and rushes to the office. This is the first time something like this has happened.

Praveen's heart is pounding so loudly that he is afraid others can hear it. They enter Ramaiah's room and wait nervously for Ramaiah to arrive. The office peon comes and greets them, gives them a glass of water, and rushes in to get the filter coffee. Usually, Praveen enjoys this routine. Usually, he has a broad smile on his face. Usually, he is very friendly to the staff. But today is completely different.

Soon, Ramaiah enters the room. Ramaiah is his enthusiastic self, greets Praveen with a smile and asks, "How have you been, Praveen? How is the new venture of yours?"

"I thought it would be a venture, but it's an adventure," says Praveen.

Ramaiah laughs out loud. Jee and Jo look at each other. In the anxiety, Praveen has blurted out the truth, and they all know it.

They finish the coffee without talking about anything substantial, just weather, politics, business conditions, etc. The deck is now clear for the actual present, which everyone has assembled there for.

Praveen takes the lead, clears his throat, and starts to speak. "LTR brand is among the top 100 most valuable brands in the country today. In fact, this is the only brand of traditional food competing for neck-to-neck with the global MNC brands. I am fortunate to be a part of this journey along with Mr Ramaiah for the last decade."

Praveen is clever enough to ensure he establishes his credentials in front of two new gentlemen in the room and reminds Ramaiah about the long association and journey. Ramaiah nods affirmatively. Jee and Jo are already bored.

"However, we know that developing a brand is not a destination but a journey. And like all other journeys, this journey is not without challenges. We need to identify them, evaluate them, and overcome them."

Praveen is explaining indirectly that whatever has happened couldn't have been avoided and he is the right person to fix it.

"About three months ago, Mr Ramaiah shared with us a challenge the LTR brand faces, which is very serious and can't be overlooked. Although LTR is the number one choice for middle-aged, traditional customers, the younger generation, who comes from the same traditional route, is not connected with the brand. The recognition is poor, they haven't experienced the brand and they consider it as 'old-fashioned,' 'parochial,' and hence, don't want to be associated with it.

"So we at Creativity Unlimited took up the challenge of repositioning the brand by communicating to the younger generation. We think the brand values are still very strong, so there is no need to change them, but we need a better digital campaign to connect with the younger customers and make ourselves relevant.

"Let me introduce my colleagues—Jyotichandrika heads the creative department and Jeetendraprasad plans the media."

Both of them greet everyone and try to smile; they manage a grimace of some sort.

"They have come up with an excellent campaign that we can launch immediately. We have worked on it together, and I am confident that you will like it."

Ramaiah has heard these lines umpteen number of times from Praveen.

"Let me request Jyotichandrika to explain the campaign to all of us. Over to you."

Jo is not used to wearing *salwar kameej*, so she is very uncomfortable in general. She clears her throat.

"Hello everyone, my name is Jyotichandrika, but please call me Jo."

Jo doesn't want to lose a chance to assert herself.

"Let me explain our idea by showing you the storyboard for the video ad first. That will make our thought process clearer."

She distributes the printout of the storyboards to everyone.

"We want to show that parents are becoming modern to connect with their kids. And how this in turn brings a positive effect on kids and they then accept their parent's choices."

Jo blurts this out loudly, albeit unconvincingly. When Praveen proposed this storyline a few weeks ago, she remembers that she had said that dudes of our generation are not idiots to accept parents' choices just because they started using Facebook. But she is forced to come up with this creative concept and pass it as if it's her own, which Praveen thinks would help them to win the account. The result is obvious: Jo is saying what Praveen wants to hear but there is no conviction.

"So, the opening scene, shows a son, twenty-five years of age, wearing cool funky clothes, sitting in his room and playing a video game. A daughter about eighteen years of age, wearing distressed jeans, watching YouTube on her phone. Their rooms are very modern and jazzy."

Ramaiah is hiding his face below his palm and looks non-committal.

"Then in the second shot, we show their mother working in the kitchen, using LTR ingredients to make laddoos and murukku. She tastes each one of them and closes her eyes. She loves the taste. She then calls out to her son and daughter, but both of them don't respond. Their father, sitting at the dining table, looks very angry and is about to get up and go to their room. The mother stops him and smiles.

"In the third shot, she pulls out her smartphone, goes to Twitter, and tweets the son and the daughter asking them to join for a snack at the dining table. She also takes a picture of the snacks and uploads it to her Facebook.

"In the final shot, both the son and daughter see the tweet, smile, and join their parents at the dining table. The entire family is relishing LTR snacks and as the branding comes in and the camera fades away, the son and daughter are seen fighting with each other for the last laddoo. The mother splits it into half, it looks to be fresh and warm as the camera goes for a long shot and they are all seen as a happy family."

Jo's description is rather engaging. Everyone can visualize the advertisement in front of their eyes. Praveen smiles ear to ear. But Ramaiah wears a poker face. Jo has done what she was supposed to do but it hasn't created a desired effect. For the last decade, by this point, Praveen would see Ramaiah's face brighten up. He would ask further questions about the background music or who would the model be. Today, his face is still shrouded in thought, expressionless. Praveen knows that he is in unknown territory.

Jo is about to start an explanation about the brand and packaging, etc. but Praveen stops her and asks Ramaiah, "How do you like it, sir?"

"It's good. Quite different than what I thought."

Ramaiah's reply is even more puzzling.

"Do you have any particular point that you want to make?" Praveen asks. He wants to get to the bottom of this.

"Well, I am not absolutely sure if the young generation would accept their parental choice just because the parents connect with them on social media," says Ramaiah.

Jo and Jee feel vindicated. They look at each other through the corner of their eyes and smile. Praveen senses this. He also remembers a rather heated discussion he had with Jo and Jee about this. Both Jo and Jee had clearly mentioned that this storyline made no sense, but it was Praveen who made them do it. Now he doesn't know how to navigate out of this.

"Let us look at the media plan before we get into the brand assets." Praveen changes the track. "Jeetendraprasad, over to you."

Jee clears his throat and says, "Hello everyone, call me Jee. If you have to take to the younger audience, you need to completely change your media selection. People of my generation don't look at billboards, they don't read the newspaper, and seldom watch TV. They are glued to their mobiles, watch YouTube, Vimeo, and play games on the screen. That is where our ad needs to appear . . . "

Praveen is growing uncomfortable with his narration, Jee is not sticking to the script. So Praveen decides to interrupt him, "What Jeetendraprasad is saying is correct, but we found that 15% of our younger customers do watch TV with their parents and that is our core segment. We will launch this advertisement on TV in the full 30-second version and then take it to YouTube,

Instagram, and other channels with a 15-second version. That we think will help us to capture the best of both worlds."

It goes without saying that Jee hasn't bought into this media plan. He thinks 30 seconds are too long and showing it on TV doesn't serve any purpose at all. He also can't imagine watching an ad that shows a woman similar to his mother, appearing on YouTube. He thinks it's a big put off. He has explained this to Praveen but clearly, Praveen is pushing his own agenda.

Praveen says, "Let me now present the brand assets that are even more exciting."

Ramaiah raises his hand and asks him to stop. Praveen's worst fears have come true. He has presented his campaign exactly the way he wanted but the result is quite the opposite. His heart sinks further.

Ramaiah says, "We have understood your approach. Frankly, I was expecting something radically different. Praveen, I have known you for over a decade, and I fully trust you. I am sure you would have done your best to come up with a radically different campaign but I can understand that it might be a challenge for you to get this young generation to follow your vision."

Ramaiah throws an unexpected lifeline at Praveen. Jo and Jee are furious. They think the world is so unfair. Left to themselves they would have created a pathbreaking campaign, but it was Praveen who stopped them. But the client is blaming them for the shortfall. So unfair!

"I will again consider your campaign but at this stage, I don't think we can go ahead," Ramaiah concludes. His assistant senses that the meeting is getting over, so he walks in with a file, which presumably has the signed contract, but Ramaiah waves at him asking him to leave the room. He walks back with the file.

The meeting is over. Ramaiah folds his hands and stands up. Red-faced, Praveen also gets up reluctantly. Jo and Jee are glad the ordeal is over.

As Praveen is walking toward the door, he notices a new poster on the wall facing Ramaiah.

'What got you here, may not take you further.'

He is aghast.

He walks to the car. Jo and Jee make some excuse not to join him in his car. They just want to flee the situation. It wasn't their fault, but they were the scapegoats.

Praveen drives out of the LTR office. One question pops up in his mind. *Will this be the last time?* Before he dwells on this question any further, his phone rings. It's Paul.

CHAPTER 11

A Small Leak Can Sink
a Great Ship

When alliances crumble and trust erodes, the
aftershocks threaten to sink the ship of success.

J o and Jee reach the office as fast as they can. They
want to tell all the buddies about the colossal failure
that was the meeting. Although they are part of the
team that should have made the meeting a success, this
failure gives them joy. They feel as if they have scored a
moral victory over Praveen.

"*Haar kar bhi jeetnewale ko baazigar kehte hai . . . kya kehte
hai? Baazigar,*" they deliver this dialogue in Shahrukh Khan's
style, and laugh.

Little do they know that this failure has the potential to
bring down the whole company in no time at all. This is like
a small innocuous-looking hole at the bottom of a big ship
that could potentially sink the whole ship.

Paul knows this. He is sitting in front of Praveen but
both haven't uttered a word for the last ten minutes.

"But you said that you have everything under control . . . " says Paul, unable to think of anything else.

"Yes, I did. But your team is totally crazy. They can't understand simple instructions. They screwed it up," says Praveen at the top of his voice.

Paul is not a man of details. He is also aware of the tiff between Praveen and the team, so this story sounds totally believable. He is also not well-equipped to probe Praveen further to find out the real reason.

"So what now? What is our next step?" Paul asks.

"Honestly, I don't know," says Praveen.

"What? How can you say this? You are in charge. We are going exactly as per your plan."

"Well, you made me captain of the ship but the crew doesn't listen to me. So either I change the crew or . . . " Praveen leaves the sentence incomplete.

"Or? Or what?" Paul is irritated now.

Praveen realizes his mistake. He shouldn't have jumped the gun and announced his intention.

"Nothing. I share an excellent relationship with Ramaiah. I will seek a one-on-one appointment with him and find out what he really wants and turn this around," Praveen says hurriedly.

"Are you sure you can salvage this?"

"Of course. I have to. Do you see any other alternative?" asks Praveen.

Paul thinks for a while and says, "No. Not really."

Praveen is happy that Paul is totally dependent on him. That's how he derives his power in every relationship. But in the heart of hearts, he is still looking for options. He knows that since he shares a good relationship with Ramaiah, he would agree to meet him. But he would never let him talk about the campaign, nor would he give him a second chance.

That is exactly how Praveen had displaced the earlier agency. Just one mistake is what it takes to lose accounts like LTR. The relationship still exists, but the business does not.

Praveen feels tired. He decides to go home. He assures Paul that he will find a solution. He thinks to himself that maybe once he cools down and sleeps over the matter, some solution will emerge. In any case, there is nothing he can do at the moment. He says goodbye to Paul and heads home. Paul decides to go to the office.

When he reaches the office, Jo and Jee are encircled by all the buddies. They are telling their stories animatedly and buddies are nodding in approval. There is a strange sense of joy and victory prevalent among the group. They don't look like a team that has just come out of the worst meeting in the history of their company. They are so engrossed that they don't notice Paul walking into the office.

Julie comes to the pantry area with the false pretense of filling up her water bottle and drives everyone away. They notice Paul and disperse to their seats. The gossiping now starts on their chat windows in silent mode.

Paul parks himself in the cabin. He asks Julie to order some food for him. He is totally unsure if he should invite Jo and Jee, and ask them about their version. In the eight months that he spent in the office, he didn't particularly build a strong rapport with them and he is not sure whether they will be honest with him. He is right. Jo and Jee neither like nor trust Paul, so they would never volunteer any information. It is a stalemate situation. Paul sits inside the cabin waiting for his food.

Suddenly, the direct line in the cabin rings. Paul is not sure if he should pick it up. But the phone display shows that the call is from Orchid Advertising, one of their important clients, so Paul answers.

"Is this Creativity Unlimited?" a receptionist asks in a very professional tone.

"Yes, it is."

"May I know who is on the line?"

"It is me, Paul, owner of this company."

"Oh, great. My MD would like to speak to you."

"But why? Err . . . hmm." Paul tries to find out more but the receptionist is in a great hurry to transfer the call.

"Hello, this is Das, MD of Orchid Advertising. Is Sid there? Oh no, he moved on, right. Then is Praveen there?"

"No, he is not in at the moment. This is Paul. I am the owner of Creativity Unlimited. You can talk to me."

"Oh, nice to meet you, Paul. I have heard a lot about you but never got a chance to talk to you. How are you?"

"I am doing great. How can I help you?" Paul is losing his patience. He knows this is not a business-as-usual call.

"I called you to inform you that we have just learned that you have approached LTR, one of the prominent food companies, to run their campaign directly. This is quite shocking. We clearly understood with Sid that they would never approach any company but only work with ad agencies like us. That was the basis on which we trusted Sid and gave so much business."

"But did we have any agreement like that?" Paul was puzzled.

"Not the legal agreement but a gentleman's agreement. We gave exclusivity to Creativity Unlimited. We would not work with any other digital agency, and in return, we would expect that Creativity Unlimited never approaches clients of any ad agency."

"But why would you make an arrangement like that?"

"Paul, you are a businessman. You know how it works. This arrangement would allow us to have the cake and eat it too. We would take care of the conventional mass media and earn our margins. In addition, we would add the digital campaigns done by your company to keep our clients happy. Clients felt they were striking the right balance. We got our money, you got yours. Everything was working so well. I don't know why you had to disturb the equilibrium?"

"But how did you know?"

"We live on the same planet, Paul. The security guard on LTR's gate has been getting Diwali gifts from Orchid Advertising for the last ten years. We know everything."

The corporate rivalry has an ugly face. It is impossible to know who is a friend and who is an enemy. Not everyone who smiles at you is a friend, and everyone who hates you is an enemy.

"So I have asked my legal team to study the exit clause in our contract. We are going to invoke it. Since we have been working for a long time, I thought I would call you and tell you before the official notice arrives at your doorstep."

"No, Mr Das. You can't do this to us."

"Oh, yes. I can do this, Paul," asserted Das. "So many digital agencies come knocking on our doors every time, but we won't let them in because we had this arrangement with you. But now that you have broken this arrangement, it's a golden chance for us to find another faster, better, and cheaper company than you."

"No, sir. You can't find such a company. Sid has built this company from scratch, and you know we are so different."

"Yes. From what I know, you were different till Sid left, but since then, I have heard that things are not going well. Praveen is struggling to establish himself. It's a turf war between him and the old guard."

If Das could find out what was happening in LTR's office, he could find out what was happening in Creativity Unlimited's office. Paul knows there is no point in refuting it.

"We will review our contract and send the notice accordingly. But we will end this relationship for sure even if it costs us money. It was nice working with you, and we wish you the best in future endeavors."

Paul could not decipher if it was genuine good wishes or a challenge laced with sarcasm.

Paul's food arrives. But he has no appetite.

Nothing is going right since this morning, he thinks to himself. *Maybe it's an inauspicious day.*

Even if the next day is auspicious, it doesn't undo everything that happened on an inauspicious day. This day is far from over. He decides not to hang around in the office and face this anymore. He leaves the cabin, and asks Julie to keep the food in the pantry. As he leaves the office, he hears both direct lines in the cabin ring, and Julie rushes to get them.

While exiting the building, he sees a couple of courier boys rush to their office with thick envelopes.

When the equilibrium is disturbed, even the strongest structure collapses under its weight. Suddenly, nothing seems right. Today was such a day at Creativity Unlimited. Paul and Praveen had disturbed the equilibrium by bypassing their loyal customers and their customers. It was a calculated risk.

If it worked, that is, if Creativity Unlimited had won the LTR account, they would have had an upper hand. But right now, they were on the receiving end on all sides. Neither did they win LTR, nor have any way to hold back the exodus of their loyal clients.

By evening, Creativity Unlimited had received termination notices from most clients. All these notices were lying on Praveen's table. Paul had fled, and Praveen was blissfully unaware. Within a few months, Creativity Unlimited resembled a rudderless ship in the high seas.

CHAPTER 12

Mayhem

Navigating through mayhem requires
strategic finesse and teamwork.

The next day, Praveen walks into the office, totally unaware of what is in store for him. As soon as he arrives, he asks Julie for a cappuccino. He is surprised to see a mess of envelopes on this table. When Julie walks in with his hot cuppa, he asks, rather irritated, "What is this? Why are there so many envelopes lying on my table? I was away for just half a day."

Julie, with a look of surprise on her face, puts his cup on his table and says, "You mean . . . you don't know anything?"

"What do I not know? What am I missing here?"

Julie doesn't want to break the bad news, so she counter-questions, "Did Paul not tell you anything?"

"What was Paul supposed to tell me?"

"He was the one who took the first call."

Praveen is losing his cool now. "First call? What was the call about?"

Julie succumbs to being the messenger. "All the ad agencies are upset that we went directly to LTR." The minute she finishes her sentence, she turns abruptly and races out of the room.

By right, Paul should have told Praveen about this the minute he received the call, and by now, a game plan should have been in place. But this is a problem way beyond Paul's capability. He has irresponsibly decided to let Praveen deal with it himself. Praveen has walked right into this trap.

By now, all the buddies are acutely aware of the situation. They know the seriousness of the issue, and they're obviously expecting their bosses, Paul and Praveen, to fix it. For the next hour or so, Praveen sits and opens envelope after envelope, reading each termination notice. He is also noting down something on the whiteboard.

Buddies are trying to get on with their work, but they have one eye on the cabin. They are anxious to know what Praveen is doing and what action he might be taking. He finishes reading all the notices and calls Julie and says, "Get me Paul. Wherever he is."

Julie understands the tone. After a few minutes, Paul is on the line.

Praveen says, "Paul, I have gone through everything. I know the gravity of the problem. We need to meet and discuss."

Paul says, "Oh okay. Then please come to the Cosmopolitan Club."

Praveen says, "No, Paul. This meeting needs to happen here in the office."

"Err . . . Hmm. Are you sure?"

"I am absolutely sure. Please come as soon as you can."

Praveen hangs up the phone. No matter what the situation

is, Praveen never ceases to show that he has the upper hand in the conversation.

He picks up the phone again and tells Julie, "Get me some sandwiches. Chicken sandwiches with Diet Coke would be fine. And yes . . . please get me a Coke can. Not the stupid bottle. Please get it fast."

By the time Praveen finishes his lunch, Paul strolls in. As he walks in, a trail of cardamom follows him. Buddies peek out of their workstations. Some of them suggest that Paul must have eaten the cardamom to mask the smell of whatever alcohol he would have had to calm his nerves.

Paul walks into the cabin. Praveen is staring at the whiteboard. On it, he has written down several statistics—how many clients Creativity Unlimited had, what was the size of the account last year, how many of them have served a termination notice, and the notice period.

Praveen turns to Paul and without any greeting or niceties, says, "Paul, this is our scoreboard. We have 22 clients, out of which 14 give us regular business. Out of these 14, 9 companies have served us a termination notice. Luckily, our notice period varies from three to six months. We have several ongoing projects, so we can sustain ourselves for three to four months."

Paul says, "That's it? What happens after that?"

"We need to win new business by then. Maybe we go back and negotiate with these nine clients and regain their business. We need to do whatever it takes to stay afloat."

Paul says, "What if we can't?"

"I don't want to even think of that possibility right now."

Paul counters, "Why don't we first try to address the LTR account where it all began. Remember you had told me once that if we won the LTR account and lost all others that is still worth it. Is that a foregone conclusion?"

Praveen, understandably, is unwilling to discuss the LTR fiasco in front of Paul. He definitely doesn't want to bring Jo, Jee, and Paul in one room. The version he has given to Paul is quite different from the reality and Paul has bought his version. If Paul insists on talking to Jo and Jee, the cracks in his narrative will be exposed. He can't take that risk.

However, Paul has a very simplistic mind. The current situation with the 9 clients who have served them with a termination notice and now how to deal with each case and how to come out of it, etc., is too complicated for him to handle. His mind is fixated on winning back LTR, which was an integral part of the plan. If that is set right, he doesn't need to deal with the entire complex situation.

So his mind insists on dealing with the LTR situation first. He stops convincing Praveen, picks up the phone and asks Julie to send Jo and Jee inside. After both of them enter the cabin, Paul asks them to grab a chair. Praveen is still trying his best to deflect the topic.

So he takes a lead and says, "At the LTR meeting yesterday, whatever happened has happened. But we are gathered here to discuss and strategize what we can do to turn things around and win back the account."

Jee quips, "Oh, that is very simple. Let me and Jo handle the campaign our way. Didn't you hear what Ram-dude said?"

There is an awkward pause. Paul is confused even more.

Paul says, "Let us start from the beginning. Can you tell me what happened at the meeting?"

Jo looks at her feet. Jee says, "Why not? Here's the deal. We had prepared the campaign exactly as per Praveen's plan. Jo and I did not fully agree with it but in our effort to be team players, we followed what Praveen said. Jo presented the campaign very well. But Ram-dude threw us out."

Paul doesn't know what to say. He realizes that this is not what Praveen has told him and wonders why Praveen is not countering this. But he is still unsure of Jo and Jee.

"What clothes were you both wearing?" Paul's investigation takes a wrong turn.

"*Chudidar*! Can you imagine?" Jo cannot maintain her silence anymore in her irritation. "I had to go to Commercial Street to buy one over the weekend."

Paul takes a good look at her. She is wearing a short top, showing off her flat stomach and belly ring, and hot pants.

"No, I can't imagine," Paul confesses.

Even amidst this tense situation, Jo and Jee laugh.

Jee says, "That was a rhetorical question, Paul."

Paul is not in a mood to ask what that meant. He looks at Jee and asks, "And you? What were you wearing?"

"Full sleeves shirt and office trousers. So embarrassing."

Since the attire box is ticked, Paul probes further. "What was the color of your hair in the meeting?"

"Same, Paul. Do you think I can change my hair color in a day?"

"I don't know. Maybe put a natural color back on green or purple whatever color you had yesterday."

"No, Paul. Nothing like that happened. We were properly attired and wore boring office going hairstyles. I told you the problem wasn't with us, it was with the campaign."

There is an awkward pause again and everyone looks expectantly at Praveen.

Clearly uncomfortable at being caught like this, Praveen clears his throat and says, "What happened yesterday at LTR was totally unprecedented. I have been dealing with Mr Ramaiah for the last ten years, but he has never responded like he did yesterday."

Jo and Jee think to themselves. *Who cares? Tell us what to do next.*

Paul is, surprisingly enough, also thinking the same thing they are.

"I think there is a significant departure from their stated needs to what they expect from the campaign. They were always a very conservative client who had shunned any pathbreaking communication approach. I am quite sure, the campaign we presented yesterday would have gone through, if I had presented it with my Urjaa team."

"Exactly, Pee," Jo says. "This is the exact problem. The expectations from us, as Creativity Unlimited, are completely different from your Urjaa Advertising. We are known to read the minds of youngsters and come up with the campaign that boardrooms may hate but youngsters love. That is what we do."

Jee added, "You made us come up with a campaign that you would like your Urjaa team to make but it won't work with us."

For the first time in the last few months, Paul actually listens to the buddies and is impressed with their thought process.

Praveen says brashly, "That is not the point. We are not here to make Ramaiah happy. We are here to build his brand and make it likeable to his target audience. Even if he doesn't like the campaign it is okay. If the ad works in the market, he will eventually like it."

Paul contemplates, "Good point. But how do you make him spend on an ad that he doesn't like?"

"Leave that to me. I will use all my rapport with him and make him do it.

Paul desperately wants something to rejoice about, so he says, "Excellent! Please go ahead. We are there to support you."

"No, Paul. I have to do this alone. I have to go there and win the battle."

The relief in the room is palpable.

"When do you plan to do it?" Paul wants to wind this up so that he can have his evening drinks without guilt.

"Let me choose the right time and place for the next meeting. I'll get back to you."

"Sure, take all the time in the world but make it happen." Paul is happy with the assurance. He doesn't need any details.

Jee says, "That's the spirit, Pee-dude. You are leading from the front. Way to go."

"Can we go now?" Jo has run out of patience and wants to get out of the room.

Both Jee and Jo are waved out of the room and as usual head downstairs for a cigarette.

Paul asks, "Praveen, what do you suggest we do about the termination notices?"

"Yes, we have to deal with that too, But that is my second priority. If we have LTR under our fold, then our bargaining position improves."

Paul is pleased to hear management jargon.

"Let me review this and return to you," concludes Praveen.

"That is excellent, Praveen. We have covered a lot of ground. I think we will recover from this situation."

Praveen senses Paul's desperation to create positivity to reduce the guilt for that evening drink.

"Why fear when I am here!" Praveen says.

Both of them laugh.

Within five minutes, Paul leaves the office and heads toward the Cosmopolitan Club.

Ten minutes later, Praveen also heads out. He has no intention of spending more time in that office. Neither does he have any purpose to counter the termination notices. He is just worried about his relationship with LTR and Ramaiah. Irrespective of what happens at Creativity Unlimited, these close personal relationships with the industry veterans are his lifelines. He is determined to save these relationships at any cost even if it means selling Creativity Unlimited down the river.

CHAPTER 13

Show Me Some Magic

Game of strategic maneuvers

Over the next few days, Praveen comes into the office at 9 a.m. sharp and sits in his cabin, rifling through all the termination notices. He then writes back to all the clients, writing letters that run into multiple pages, and asks Julie to send the printed copies over by courier. Paul calls him once in a while and Praveen promptly reports to him that he is waiting for the right time to re-approach Ramaiah and that he is not wasting any time to get the termination situation under control.

The reality, however, is that Praveen is still thinking about what he should say to Ramaiah before he can even consider meeting him. The long letters he is sending to the clients are merely clarifications in the termination notices that can't even buy him more time, never mind winning back the clients. He's just trying to keep up with appearances to figure out how to restore the relationship with Ramaiah and then, as a last priority, MAYBE salvage the situation for Creativity Unlimited.

In evidence of how smart he can be, he asks Julie to connect him to LTR at least three to four times a day, and he spends this time speaking to various people across the organization. In his time with that company, he has met many people across the hierarchy. They may not have any influence on what is happening, but they oblige Praveen with the latest news.

He learns about the whereabouts of Ramaiah, the latest problems LTR faces, and, most importantly, the status of other agencies meeting with LTR. All this intelligence comes in handy when he has occasional conversations with Paul about LTR.

He can say things like, "Mr Ramaiah is very concerned about the performance of the eastern region. So he has gone to Kolkata for ten days. He plans to visit the field."

Or he can mention, "The market outstanding from distributors has crossed 90 days of sales, so the entire organization is focused on recovery."

This reassures Paul that Praveen is on the job to get inside LTR.

He was trying his luck and following the strategy—fake it till you make it.

After a couple of weeks, he finally mustered up enough courage to call Ramaiah and asked him for an appointment. Ramaiah obliges. Praveen has a plan.

As usual, he pulls over his BMW in front of the LTR office. The security guard removes the reserved board and salutes Praveen. Praveen approaches him with a nervous smile and says in broken Kannada, *"Utta ayata?"* (Did you have your lunch?) And proceeds to Ramaiah's cabin without waiting for an answer. He keeps tapping his fingers on the desk while waiting for Ramaiah to arrive. Soon, Ramaiah comes with his signature enthusiasm and broad smile. He signals for filter coffee.

"How is your family? Are they happy with your new job?" Ramaiah asks.

Praveen is startled as this is the first time in the last ten years that Ramaiah has mentioned his family. Small talk is usually about Praveen's job, interesting campaigns, or politics.

"Yes, they are very happy because now I can go back on time."

Both of them laugh.

"How is business looking?"

Since Praveen hasn't met any clients in the last month or so, he doesn't know the market gossip but he sits back with a general answer. "Looking up. If we have a good monsoon, the rural economy would get a boost which would be good for all of us."

These are some general trends that are always true.

They go through their usual filter coffee dance—Praveen appreciates it, Ramaiah appreciates his appreciation.

The stage is now set for Praveen to perform his magic.

Praveen says, "Mr Ramaiah, we have been working with each other for the last decade or so, but I don't recall a single time where my campaign got rejected like it did a few days ago. May I know what was wrong?"

Ramaiah said, "It did have a fresh look and the storyline was quite different and modern. I must say it had that Praveen-touch."

Ramaiah felt compelled to compliment. Praveen nods with a smile.

"However, I feel it will not change the perception about our brand. I don't think it will help us to attract younger customers."

Praveen sees a way out.

Praveen says, "Mr Ramaiah, am I right to say that you have trusted me for the last ten years?"

"Yes, of course."

"And am I right to say that you have benefitted from my contribution to your brand?"

"Yes. Without a doubt."

"And would you say, I would be counted as one the biggest well-wishers of the LTR brand?"

"Yes, of course."

"And would I be right to say that my knowledge about your brand personality, brand values is one of the best?"

"Totally agreed, Praveen."

"Then would you trust my judgment about the LTR brand and its future?"

"That I would."

Ramaiah has fallen into a classic Praveen trap. He asks obvious questions and gets the other person to say 'Yes' a number of times and then slips a question he wants them to answer affirmatively. He has never failed.

Praveen smiles victoriously. He's found a way. It's a risky move, but the risk would be borne by Creativity Unlimited and not Praveen. He would escape unscathed if it doesn't work, but would benefit the most if it does.

He says, "Mr Ramaiah, I am very confident that the campaign we showed you last week is perfect and it will work. I am quite sure it would improve your perception among young customers."

Ramaiah doesn't look convinced but says, "I am listening."

Praveen says, "I suggest we run this campaign for a period of three months as per our media plan. You should ask your research agency to monitor the panel of young customers on a monthly basis. If we see more than a 15% increase in a positive predisposition toward your brand, then we should consider this campaign successful and you should award us the contract. If it doesn't, we will quietly withdraw."

Ramaiah seems pleased but adds, "If you are so confident about the campaign, I suggest you should accept my condition that we will pay you only if the campaign is successful. If not, you pay for the campaign."

This was the trickiest condition ever. But Praveen doesn't think much. He sees an escape route and he decides to take it.

"Done, sir," he says.

Ramaiah smiles agreeably. "Praveen, on this note, let us have one more coffee. What do you say?"

"I was about to say the same thing."

Ramaiah uncharacteristically steps out to order coffee and returns after five minutes. Praveen is so happy with the turn of events that he doesn't stop to think about this.

Soon, Ramaiah's cabin is filled with the aroma of filter coffee. It is served in two steel glasses. Praveen picks it up and takes a sip.

They again talk about politics and related topics over coffee. As Praveen is about to leave, Ramaiah's clerk walks in with a piece of paper. He has drafted a simple agreement, based on Ramaiah's instructions, that LTR is liable to pay for the campaign only if it works. Praveen had not expected paperwork and proof of this agreement but he is in no position to argue. He signs it with a smile, and even Ramaiah is fooled by his show of confidence.

Praveen brushes aside all negative thoughts, gets up, folds his hands at Ramaiah and leaves the office. As he reaches his car, he calls Paul and asks to meet at the Cosmopolitan Club.

"Cheers!" Both Praveen and Paul say together.

"Congratulations on winning back LTR, Praveen." Paul is more relieved than happy.

"Thank you. Thanks for keeping the faith in me and not listening to the crap that Jeetendraprasad was blurting out."

"No, no. Not at all. I trust you."

"Thanks."

"But tell me, how did this happen? What magic did you do?"

"That's my professional secret." Praveen laughs out loud. "But on a serious note, Ramaiah has thrown a challenge at us. I think he wants to see how confident we are in our campaign and maybe I missed this trick of his the last time. Today, I vouched for our campaign wholeheartedly."

"That is fantastic!"

"Ramaiah wanted my personal guarantee that it would work. He was asking if their acceptance would increase by at least 10%. I said I can guarantee 15%. He was very pleased; couldn't wait to sign us on!"

"That is terrific. This is what the young generation of Jyoti, Jeetendra, and Sid should learn from you. You know how to handle even the most difficult client."

Paul was singing praises. Praveen continued to brush away any nagging doubts at the back of his mind.

The next day, Praveen calls Jo and Jee to his cabin as soon as he reaches office. He announces that he had a very successful meeting with Ramaiah. He tells them that Ramaiah has completely empowered him to decide on the campaign, media plan and budget. He gives them appropriate instructions and asks them to get back to him by the end of the day.

Jo and Jee can feel that something is amiss but follow Praveen's instructions anyway. Jee brings the media plan for Praveen's approval. Praveen approves it promptly.

"Should I mail it to Ramaiah's office for invoicing?"

"No, no. We will bill them at the end of three months, altogether."

"Really? Are you sure?"

"Of course. That is a standard process in all ad agencies."

"Really? Sorry we didn't know. We are used to invoicing clients on day one."

"No worries. Now that I am here, I will help you to implement all new practices. I will also negotiate a longer credit period with the media. So our company won't be burdened."

"Thanks a lot. That's very thoughtful."

"No worries."

"Should I just send a copy to Ramaiah for his information?"

"No, no. There is no need. He has fully empowered me to make decisions."

"Great then."

Jee wants to talk to Jo about this turn of fortune.

"Dude, something doesn't seem right," says Jee.

"Ya, man! Something is definitely wrong. I can feel it in my bones," Jo agrees.

"That Ram-dude threw us out of his office like just 15 days ago and now suddenly he gives complete authority to Pee-dude to spend?"

"As if he just handed him a signed blank cheque."

"This only happens in movies, man, like bad movies."

"Do you think we are being taken for a ride? Should we ask someone?" Jo's brows are creased with concern.

"If that is the case it's going to be the most expensive ride in the whole wide world." Jee is not sure what else he can say. "Let us hope we are wrong," he continues.

"I hope so, too. I miss Sid."

"Me too! Big time!"

"If he was around, nothing like this would have happened. No games, no complications. Just work and loads of fun."

"I wonder what he is up to. Do you know?" Jee asks.

"Nope," says Jo.

Their cigarette crumbles into ash and both of them rush back.

CHAPTER 14

What Is Sid Up To?

In the company of excellence: oneself.

Eight months ago

Sid wakes up, rushes through his daily chores, and starts to make himself a cup of tea, and stops short when he realizes that there is no need to rush anymore. He doesn't need to go anywhere. This is something he has never felt. For the last eight years, he has always sprung out of bed, rushed through the morning routine and reached the office, all at breakneck speed. Now he doesn't have to. Now, he has to find a new routine.

Ever since he passed his Post Graduate Diploma course from the Indian Institute of Management, Bangalore, he has had a single-minded focus on Creativity Unlimited. He had no time to keep in touch with his friends, nor time to make new ones.

He lives in the sleepy neighborhood of RT Nagar, on the first floor of a typical Bangalore house. The ground floor is occupied by his landlord and his wife. Their son and daughter both are living abroad. Sid is a good tenant, pays rent on time, is away most of the time, doesn't have many visitors and he also has the same name as their son so the landlord is very happy to have him as a tenant.

The landlady sends some *dosai* or *bisi bele bath* for Sid when she misses her son. But beyond that, they don't know much about Sid's life.

On that day, while sipping the tea that he made without a time limit, Sid realizes how lonely he is.

He finishes his tea and reaches out to his phone.

"Hello, ma. *Kaisi ho aap?*"

Sid's mother is surprised to get his call at this hour. This has never happened since Sid left home for his higher education.

She asks, "*Main theek hoon bete. Aap kaise ho? Is time pe kaise phone kiya? Tabiyat theek hai aap ki?*"

Sid says, "*Haan, ma, main theek hoon.*"

Indian mothers have a sixth sense of their offspring. So she is not convinced.

"*Bukhar to nahi hain?*"

"*Nahi, ma, main bilkul theek hoon.*"

"*Kya khaya aapne nashte mein?*"

Sid senses that his mother is going to start a detailed diagnostic process to solve the mystery of his impromptu phone call. Indian mothers believe that the clues to such quests lie in what their kids eat, so she wants to check on the last consumed meal.

Sid doesn't want to walk into that trap. His mother has not accepted his decision to go to South India to study or that he's working there, so telling her that he had a South-Indian meal for breakfast would not be in his best interests. He changes tack.

"*Aap ki bahut yaad aa rahi thi, ma.*"

"Aww, that is so sweet." Sid hears the emotion quavering in her voice. After a few moments of silence, his mother's investigation begins again.

"*Kuchh paise chahiye kya aap ko, beta?*"

"*Nahi, ma. Aisi koi baat nahi hai. Paise bahot hai mere paas.*"

"*Acha theek hain, mera mann rakhne ke liye paanch hazar aap mujhse le hi lo.*"

Sid's attempts to have a normal conversation with his mother are thwarted by her determination to investigate the reason behind this unexpected phone call.

"*Iski koi jarurat nahi hain, ma. Paise hain mere paas.*"

"*Acha to main samajh gayi. batao batao ladki ka naam kya hai?*"

"*Kaunsi ladki? Aap kya bol rahe ho, ma?*"

"*Sharmao mat. Bata do. Main kuch nahi kahungi. Fauran haan kar dungi.*"

"*Nahi ma aisi koi baat nahi hai.*"

Irritation creeps into Sid's voice. He is happy to hear his mother's voice but any dialogue beyond that does not seem feasible.

"*Hana theek hain, ma. Mujhe dusara call aa raha hai. Main baad me phir se call karta hoon. Pitaji ko pranam kehna.*"

Sid hangs up. Some wishes are simple but not easy. It's just half past 9 and he has a full day ahead of him. And then many more days till he finds what he is going to do next.

He looks around at his room. It is a mess. A maid comes in to come and clean the room but she doesn't touch his clothes, trophies, or books, which are strewn about. The wall hanging is old. The photo frames are gathering dust. The first order of business can be to clean up the place then. He picks up the books and arranges them in the bookcase by the author. He finds gift-wrapped packages lying around and opens them to find well-known titles he's always been meaning to read.

He re-arranges his trophies—most of them are from his college days and a few plaques that he has received as head of Creativity

Unlimited. He finds a cleaning cloth and starts cleaning the photo frames. Most of the frames are from his college days. The frame at the top shows his graduation photograph, arguably the proudest moment of his life. Then some photographs in their hostel rooms, some in the mess, and then there is also the photograph from a picnic in Coonoor.

He cleans this photo really well and holds it close. In it, Anjali is standing right next to him, just as she always did through all his college days. Whenever he needed her, she was always right there. Sid was the one who failed her.

"I want to be someone in terms of my career then think about love and settling down," Sid remembers him saying this to Anjali in the concluding days of their college.

"I'm not going to stop you from achieving anything! I could be your mental support," pleaded Anjali.

"Yes, you are, you will be, but it's not you; it's me. With you around, I won't be focused. I will feel distracted."

"So what are you saying?"

"I will stay put in Bangalore to see if something can be done with my business idea. Yesterday, I got a call from someone named Paul, who said he is impressed with my idea and wants to meet me. Maybe something will work out."

"Sid, think again. I have got a great job in Delhi. If you try a little harder here or stay with me in Delhi, you will easily find a great job. We have a great career ahead of us. And we can be together, too. Don't spoil it, Sid. We can do both, career and our life." Anjali holds his hands and tries to look into his eyes.

Sid cannot meet her gaze.

"No, Anjali. I think you should take the opportunity and go to Delhi. I am sure you will do well. I am not going away. There is no other girl in my life. Obviously, we will stay in touch and, eventually, get married one day."

"Get married one day?" Anjali says mockingly. "We have a long way to go, Sid!"

Anjali storms out.

Sid doesn't budge, nor does Anjali give up on her career opportunity.

Both of them, being strong individuals, happily accept the challenges of a long-distance relationship. They call each other regularly. Send pictures. Whenever Anjali takes a vacation to meet her parents, a few days are reserved for Sid. They stay together. Go on dates. Watch movies together. Very rarely, when Sid travels back home, he does the same. He visits Anjali in Delhi. They go around site seeing. Explore new places.

Any long-distance relationship goes through its ups and downs. Theirs is no exception. Sid's single-minded focus on Creativity Unlimited means Anjali has to do more than her fair share to keep up the relationship. Sid is aware of this but unable to help. Anjali, therefore, feels even more exhausted and needs him to meet more frequently and spend more time with her.

Three years ago, they had planned to go on a bike trip to Ladakh. Anjali had planned the itinerary. She spent all the time after office hours researching each and every monastery and place of interest in Ladakh. She had planned places where they would halt. Everything. Sadly, Sid cancels on her at the last moment. Anjali is still mad at him about that.

Things have not been the same between them ever since then.

Sid still doesn't have any other girl in his life, he still wants to marry Anjali, but clearly hasn't kept in touch as well as he should have.

He finishes cleaning his room. As he sits down, he looks up at the clock; it is only 10:30 a.m. He still has a full day ahead of him. With just a thought, he picks up the phone and dials Anjali's number. She hangs up. He looks at his phone, shakes his head, and calls again. This time, she picks up and says in a clipped manner, "Hi, Sid, I have to call you back. I am in a meeting." She hangs up before he can answer.

He takes a shower. By the time he gets out, Anjali calls back.

"How are you, Sid? Long time no see, no talk."

"I am okay, Anjali. How are you?"

"I am good. A lot of work and travel, which is a good sign."

"Yes, indeed."

"How are you holding up, Sid? I read an article about your company, particularly about your exit. Was it as ugly as they made it sound?"

"Frankly, I haven't read anything yet. But it wasn't fun, for sure. It feels like one part of my body has detached from me."

"What are your plans now?"

"I don't know. I haven't decided yet. I was thinking if I could . . ."

"Come and stay with me like you promised three years ago?"

"Oh, you remember?"

"Everything."

"I know, you've always had a good memory. Like an elephant, I used to say."

"Yes, that joke is just as funny as it always was."

"Can I? Can I come and see you? Can I come and stay with you?"

"No, Sid, you can't stay with me now. I am seeing someone."

Sid takes a minute to digest this. Of course she's seeing someone. Why wouldn't someone want to date her.

"Can I at least come and see you? Just as a friend."

"Just one coffee."

"Great."

"When?"

"Soon. I will book the flight and let you know."

Anjali's promise to meet him for coffee is sufficient to make him smile.

He picks up the phone and calls the travel agent.

Sid is waiting impatiently in a Cafe Coffee Day for Anjali to arrive. He hasn't entirely digested the news of her seeing someone else, but he's trying not tooverthink about that. He looks around. The metro has changed Delhi a lot. Anjali has asked him to meet at this place so she can quickly meet him and head back.

He sees her from a distance. She looks even more beautiful. From her hair to her clothes to her accessories, everything is impeccable. She walks in and stands in front of Sid. Sid almost reaches out to give her a hug, but she quickly extends her hand instead. They shake hands awkwardly, order coffee and sit down.

Anjali takes a sip of her coffee, sits back, and asks, "How was your flight? Where are you staying?"

Sid doesn't have time for formalities. He is impatient. He asks, "Who is he? Do you love him?"

Anjali raises an eyebrow and says, "I am not going to answer any of these questions. I am not answerable to you anymore."

"I know. You are not. Especially after what I did to you."

"I don't feel sad anymore, Sid. So it's okay. You had a choice to make and so did I."

Sid tries to reach out and hold her hand. Anjali jerks her hand back.

"I know."

"I did wait for you for a long time. But at some point I had to move on, right? It wasn't fair to me and it was affecting me negatively."

Anjali's eyes sparkle with a hint of tears. Sid looks down and offers his handkerchief. Anjali pretends not to notice and uses tissues instead.

"I know. I am not going to defend myself. I had my own issues to deal with but I wasn't there for you."

"Sameer was. He waited patiently for me. He waited till I could get over you. He made no other moves and allowed me to have my space. We just started dating six months ago. I'm not going to spoil it."

"I understand," says Sid hesitantly, ashamed.

"I did love you with all my heart and soul."

"So did I," says Sid.

Anjali scoffs. "I was really hoping that we would be able to do the bike trip to Ladakh that you promised me. I was really hoping to spend quality time with you and hoped that you would propose to me during that trip."

"I'm sorry. That wasn't to be. I messed up, Anjali."

"I know, Sid."

"I am sorry," says Sid, again.

"It is alright. I am over it," says Anjali.

"I am not," says Sid, hoping she can see the desperation in his face.

"But I can't help you now," says Anjali.

Sid feels as if he is shouting at the top of his voice but nobody can hear anything. He feels totally helpless. He says bye to Anjali and leaves.

Sid feels empty inside. Their relationship had soured after the Ladakh incident. But he always thought that he would be able to patch up and win her back. That is how it has always happened in the past. He realizes that he has made a big blunder by taking Anjali for granted. He reckons that she must have got tired of holding her end of the bargain.

He should have struck a balance. He should have given her the quality time she deserves. Looking back, he realizes that maybe he could have easily taken more breaks and met Anjali.

There is absolutely no excuse for not calling her once a week. He chased his dream relentlessly and lost a beautiful relationship in the real world. He knows that he has to do something about this.

Earlier, his plan was to see Anjali and then head home to Lucknow. He has let his mom know too. But this meeting with Anjali has changed everything. He has to do something to fill the void inside.

As he sips the rest of the coffee and thinks, he gets a crazy idea. If things were alright between them till he missed the trip to Ladakh, maybe he should go to Ladakh now and see if things change. Impulsively, Sid decides to go to Ladakh.

He calls Anjali.

"Anjali, don't walk away from me, please. We can still set it right."

"Do you really think so?"

"Yes, I am very sure. I still love you the same."

"But I don't."

"Are you sure? Then why did you come to see me?"

There is a long pause.

Sid says, "Let us go to Ladakh now. I will cancel all my plans to go to Lucknow. Let us do the bike trip exactly as you had planned."

"It's too late, Sid. I can't go with you."

Anjali hangs up the phone.

Sid is a little disappointed but he decides to go ahead with his bike trip plan anyway. *Maybe that will fill the void inside*, he thinks to himself. He buys a riding jacket, a riding bag, a helmet, and sunglasses. Then he rents a brand new bullet to go to Leh. He goes through his old emails and digs out Anjali's bike trip plan. He decides to follow it to the letter.

Sid sets off toward Chandigarh. Newly built national highways are in good condition. He keeps a steady speed of 60–80 kilometers per hour and rides safely in the left lane. His mind wanders, and he starts thinking deeply to understand his situation. In the last month or so, everything about his life has changed. He has lost his job without any clear plan on what to do next. He is very well-known in the industry.

In the past seven years, he has disrupted many businesses. So he has more foes than friends in the industry. Additionally, the news of his dismissal from Creativity Unlimited has been covered in the business media publications. A lot of details have found their way to the press, so Sid suspects that someone has leaked the news. It is definitely not Paul. So he wonders who it could have been.

He can't help but feel that removing him was a big setup. He is quite sure that this is Praveen's brainchild but since Paul hasn't announced any future plans he doesn't know how Praveen would gain from this. He cannot believe that he would not be part of Creativity Unlimited anymore. He's feeling quite lost.

He stops at a roadside *dhaba* for lunch. He orders butter chicken and roti with lassi. A waiter brings over the hot chicken curry and tandoor-fresh bread and keeps it in front of him. He then takes out a slab of Amul butter and puts it on top of chicken curry. The butter melts in a few seconds and an appetizing aroma engulfs Sid. He stops calculating the calories that he would consume and digs into the roti.

The waiter keeps serving him *rotis,* and he keeps eating. He loses count of the *rotis*. It is a roadside *dhaba* meant for truck drivers. The usual practice is they take a nap after lunch before they proceed. Sid realizes that he is not on a tight schedule, so he also decides to take a nap. Just a few days ago, this was inconceivable. Every minute, every second of his life was planned, but it is not anymore.

So he lies down on the *khat*—a traditional wooden bed made with woven ropes—just for the sake of it. He actually falls asleep amidst the cacophony of honking trucks, shouting drivers and dhaba workers. He wakes up after a couple of hours. For the first time in a while, his mind feels calm. He has started discovering the better side of being on a break from his career. He has a hot cup of masala chai and continues his journey.

He arrives in Chandigarh in the evening and checks into a modest hotel. He steps out for dinner in Palika Bazar sector 19. He sits quietly on a bench amidst the hustle-bustle. He sees people around him shopping, eating, laughing, and generally having a good time. Spending some time there lifts Sid's spirits. By 10 PM, the shoppers start to return back home and shops start to close down. Sid strolls back to his hotel. He absentmindedly flicks through some news and sports channels before going to bed.

Over the next couple of days, he travels from Chandigarh to Leh. The drive is wonderful. The beauty of the Himalayas is mesmerising. The stunning blue sky is littered with a few white clouds. Tall snow-clad peaks seem to pierce through them. The sunlight and shadows on these peaks create a phenomenal mosaic.

Just below the snow peaks, there is a green patch of pine trees. Below that there are cliffs that are almost vertical. And down below that, is a river flowing through the valley. One may or may not be able to see the river from each turn but you can certainly listen to the constant sound of flowing water. This collage of natural colors is strewn with small villages built on mountain slopes. They are the testimony of human determination to withstand adversities and make a good life.

Some villages look so pretty that Sid thinks that he should go and settle down in that village and write a book, learn yoga or just spend his life amidst this serene natural beauty. He keeps riding his bike and the landscape around him keeps changing. The natural beauty around him makes him miss Anjali even more. *This bike ride would be nothing short of heaven only if I had Anjali with me*, he thinks to himself.

When he enters Ladakh, the landscape transforms. Ladakh is located above the treeline—an imaginary line above which trees find it hard to survive due to lack of oxygen. In some mountains, this line is clearly visible. There are only short shrubs and grass above the treeline. Sid is amazed at the natural wonders. His mind is now occupied with different thoughts and the disappointments and frustrations seem to fade into the background. Memories of good times spent with Anjali is the cool breeze that calms his mind.

By the time he reaches near Leh, all the trees, grass, and shrubs have disappeared. He can only see brown colored soil and gray colored rocks. The roads are excellent and the presence of the Indian Army is evident. There is a chill and dryness in the air. He had read that Ladakh is a cold desert. Now he can actually experience it. On the way, he sees a board called "Magnetic Hill".

There are a lot of cars and bikes parked there. He takes a short break and tries to find out what people are doing. He asks around. People tell him that it's a place of natural wonder where the bikes or cars seem to travel upward on the slope. Usually, he would have dismissed this as some weird delusion but now he has a lot of time. So he follows what people ask him to do. He stops his bike at a place facing the upward slope, switches off the engine and puts his feet up.

To his surprise, the bike actually starts moving up the slope. It gathers some speed. People around him clap and encourage him. He poses for some pictures as a joke. He spends an hour there amidst unknown people doing seemingly meaningless things. All his life he has always been focused on solving problems, dealing with stress. Being among unknown people and doing fun things helps him to distress.

Then he rides further toward Leh. On the way, he sees a Gurdwara marked by Anjali on this map. It was Gurdwara Patthar Sahib. If he had come with Anjali, she would have explained the uniqueness of the Gurdwara. She must have done a thorough research and would have sounded like an expert. But now Sid has no other choice but to refer to Wikipedia for quick information.

According to a local legend, once a wicked demon lived in the area who terrorized the people where the gurdwara is now situated. The people prayed to the Almighty for help. It is said that Guru Nanak heard their woes and came to their aid. He settled down on the bank of the river below the hill where the wicked demon lived.

The Guru blessed the people with sermons and became popular in the area. The locals called him Nanak Lama. Seeing this, the demon got into a rage and decided to kill Guru Nanak Dev.

One morning, when the Guru was sitting in meditation, the demon pushed a large patthar (boulder), down from the hilltop, with the intention of killing the Guru. The boulder gained speed as it rumbled down the hillside, but when it touched the Guru's body, it softened like warm wax and came to a halt against Guru Nanak's back. The Guru kept on meditating, unhurt and undisturbed.

Thinking that the Guru had been killed, the demon came down but was taken aback to see the Guru deep in meditation. In a fit of anger, he tried to push the boulder with his right foot, but as the patthar still had the softness of warm wax, his foot got embedded in it. Pulling his foot out from the boulder, the demon was dumbfounded to see the impression his foot had just left in the stone.

On seeing this, the demon realized his own powerlessness in comparison to the spiritual power of the great Guru. He fell at the feet of Guru Nanak Dev and begged for forgiveness. Guru Sahib advised him to get rid of his wicked ways and asked him to lead a life of a noble person. This changed the life of the demon who gave up evil deeds and started serving the people.

Guru Nanak Dev thereafter continued his holy journey toward Srinagar via Kargil. The patthar pushed down by the demon, with the imprint of the body of Guru Nanak Dev and the footprint of the demon, is at present on display in Gurdwara Patthar Sahib. It is said that since the visit of Guru Sahib (in 1517) to the building of the roadway in 1965, the local Lamas had held the patthar sacred and offered prayers to it as, no doubt, they do to this day.

Although the story is filled with superstition, he is enthused. He parks his bike, removes his shoes, washes his feet and covers his head with the cloth provided as he enters the Gurudwara. It has a calming influence on him. He sees the large boulder with a depression that looks like a giant foot. *Maybe there are things that I don't fully understand*, he thinks to himself. Every Gurudwara always serves some food. He takes the *prasad* and quietly sits in a corner and eats it.

Sid is neither religious person nor is he an atheist. He believes that everything can be explained by clear logic and scientific principles. He doesn't oppose the concept of God or superior power that controls the universe, but doesn't really think he needs God for his problems. He's been known to say jokingly, "God has so many people to look after, why don't I look after myself so that I can reduce his workload?"

So, he has never spent much time in temples or tried to find his peace there. But here, 25 kilometres away from Leh, in a remote Gurudwara, sitting in a corner and eating the prasad, he feels peaceful. He is finding that he is able to overcome his negativity and come to terms with his present.

By evening, he reaches his hotel. It is a three-storey building and his room is on the third floor. Due to the high altitude, it is not easy to climb floors. He gets tired after climbing two stories. The hotel has provided a couch there in case of such an eventuality. He rests there for a couple of minutes and heads up to his room. The bell boy carrying his bag runs up the stairs, keeps the stuff and runs down.

Sid thinks to himself, *Maybe acclimatization makes all the difference, be it the high altitude or adverse situation.*

The next few days, Sid drove around Leh, visiting different monasteries. Every day is a new day for Sid. He gets up with a fresh mind, makes his plans, and tries to follow them as much as possible. If he can't complete them, he does them the next day. He mingles with locals. Eats at modest roadside joints. Sees the daily struggles of life people there face. It is a humbling experience.

On the way to Thiksey monastery, he sees a natural wonder that they call moon land—a patch of land that looks like land on the moon. He visits the Padma Karpo school, which is featured in the movie *3 Idiots* as Rancho's school. The school is famous for practical, micro-inventions designed to make the lives of common people in the region easier. *There is so much happening in the world. What I am doing is a minuscule portion. I think that I have changed the world but it has no relevance to these people. Their lives are totally different.*

He spends some time in the monastery. He discovers the calming influence the Buddha has on everyone. By now, the entire hotel staff knows him. They know what he likes for breakfast and dinner. If he is late, they wait for him and ensure he gets hot meals.

Then, he rides up to Khardung La, the highest motorable pass in the world. They say it is dangerous to stay there for more than twenty minutes. He buys a small souvenir from the gift shop and proceeds to the valley. The weather is wonderful and riding a bike amidst nature is liberating. He travels toward Nubra valley. He stops in a makeshift camp near Nubra valley.

Locals tell him to visit the sand dunes for a camel ride. He is surprised to hear that there are camels at this altitude. He wants to go and see it for himself. He reaches the sand dunes and finds double hump camels. *We don't know much about the world,* he thinks to himself. He takes a ride on the camel. He asks locals where these camels come from and how they survive at this altitude.

The locals share an interesting story with him. They say, "Ladakh was an important connector to the ancient silk route, the route used by Chinese and Indian traders to take silk to the Middle East, Asia, and Europe. The traders would use camels to transport their goods. Some of those camels escaped or were abandoned. They made this valley their home. Now they live there."

Sid asks, "But how do you afford to keep them throughout the year? Tourists would come only during summer, right?"

The camel owner says, "Of course. We can't afford to keep them for the whole year. After the tourist season, we abandon them. They go and live in jungles for the rest of the year. Before the tourist season, we go to jungles and catch them again."

Sid asks, "But the jungle is so big. How do you catch them?"

The camel owner says, "It is all about food, sir. We go to jungles and leave their favorite food and catch them. Some experienced camels return on their own."

He takes a glance at the camels and says, "Maybe they like this life, too."

These simple conversations help Sid to break his chain of negative thoughts. They help him heal. He can't help but imagine what would have happened if Anjali was there with him. Anjali is a person who likes stability in all aspects of her life. She can't tolerate anything shaky or unstable. It would've been fun to watch her scream and panic while riding the camel. He smiles wryly.

He travels further and reaches Pangong Tso. There is a line of tents pitched right next to the amazing lake. It looks serene.

Nature is a magician, Sid thinks to himself. At the height of 4,300 metres, there exists a lake that is 134 kilometres long. He rents a tent all for himself, puts a chair outside the tent and watches the lake. The lake changes its colors every now and then. Some patches look green, others look blue and then there are transitions from one color to another.

It is all very mystical. Sid decides to go into the lake. He dips his toes in the water. The water is freezing and sends shivers up his spine. He bends down and takes some water in his hands and splashes it on his face. He gets a taste of it, and is surprised that it's salty.

Why is the water salty? Doesn't it come from melting glaciers? Why would it lose its sweetness and become salty? Sid thinks to himself.

As Sid is strolling along the lake, he sees a group of tourists around a scooter. It is the scooter used in the movie *3 Idiots* by the character Pia, played by Kareena Kapoor. An enterprising local youth has placed a similar looking scooter and red helmet with Pangong Tso as a backdrop. He is charging Rs. 50 for a photograph on the scooter with a helmet. It is a meaningless activity and Sid otherwise would not do it, but now he is in a different frame of mind. He pays Rs. 50 to the local youth and clicks some photos. He is amused.

Back to the tent for dinner, he does ask the locals about the salty water.

The local manager says, "This water is stagnant, sir. It doesn't feed into any river or stream. You will be surprised, but such a big lake doesn't have any fish. Water is at its best when it flows, sir. If the water is stagnant, it turns salty and nobody can benefit from it."

Sid finds this profound.

Why just water, even life is at its best when it is flowing, Sid thinks to himself.

Maybe I was stagnant in Creativity Unlimited. Maybe I was turning salty. Maybe I was losing all the sweetness in me. Maybe I should start flowing again and be useful to the world.

Anjali would have been proud of this thought.

The human mind works in ways we can't imagine. Sid never thought that this unplanned trip to Ladakh would be his redemption from depressing thoughts. He never thought that praying to unknown Gods, mingling with unknown people and living at an unknown place with no fixed agenda would have had such a profound positive impact on him. While riding his bike alone for miles and miles, he thinks about Anjali all the time. Even after hearing from her that she has already moved on and started seeing someone else.

"She may have moved on, but I haven't. That is my reality," he says to himself.

After spending three weeks in Ladakh, he feels calm. He feels that the unknown void is filled to great extent. He decides to go home to Lucknow.

On his last day, he walks to the main market road in Leh. Street vendors are selling exotic fruits. He buys some apricots to munch on. He buys some T-shirts, a scarf for his mother, a winter cap for his father and a few small gifts for the hotel staff. He knows the price vendors are charging is too high, but he doesn't haggle. They smile and give him free goodies.

He thanks the hotel staff and loads his bike. The waiter runs out of the kitchen with a lunch box for Sid. They are overwhelmed with his gifts so they pack a nice lunch for him. Sid is touched. Heartfelt goodbyes are said all around. It is time to go home.

This Ladakh trip has helped him in more ways than one.

Sid reaches home, exhausted. His mother is clearly excited to see him, but she gestures to him to remove his shoes and stand outside. Sid sighs but knows he has to comply. His mother hurries out with her puja thali and does her rituals. These are the same rituals mothers would do in the olden days when their sons would come back from the war. Sid is irked but knows better than to argue.

Finally, he is let in with a hug. His father is standing right there. Sid tries to touch his feet but his father reaches down and hugs him instead. He gets another hug from his mother.

"You have come home after a long time," his father says as Sid settles into the house. His mom goes into the kitchen to prepare some food.

"Yes, father. I was really busy with my work," Sid says.

"How is work now, Sid?" his father asks again. He senses something is amiss.

"Mom, can you join us?" Sid calls out. His mother stops cooking, washes her hand and comes out to the living room.

"Dad, Mom, as you know I did really well with my company. The company grew phenomenally. I also received many awards. All my buddies loved me. But promoters for the company perhaps didn't like it. They had other ideas. So we parted ways."

"Parted ways? *Matlab*?" his mother is impatient. "It's still your company right?"

"Yes and no, Mom. Yes, I am still a part-owner of the company, but no, I can't work there anymore," Sid says feebly.

His mother doesn't understand. She starts looking at his father, worried.

His father is also trying to grapple with the situation.

"Beta, main samjha nahi, theek se samjhao?"

"Well, Papa, the promoters of the company wanted to do business in a certain way. I didn't agree because I felt my team was not ready for that and would fail miserably. I tried to convince them but they had someone else, who was advising them otherwise. It seems to me that finally the promoter listened to him."

"Okay. Now it is clear. So what did they do to you?"

"So they asked me to resign and I did. There was no point to stay and fight."

"How is that possible? You started this company, you grew this company, you're the one who worked hard. How can they remove you like this?"

"Papa, they can. It was written in my contract. They paid me for that."

"*Phir bhi, beta.* You didn't even come home for Diwali. You have given a lot to this company," his father argues.

"*Aur to aur wo Anjali ko bhi mana kiya. Us bechari ka bhi dil tod diya.* You never came home after that." His mother clearly has some information about Sid's life.

"Yes, Mom. That was the time when we were really growing and the company needed me to be there," Sid says.

"Exactly. You were there when they needed you. How can they just ask you to leave and how can you accept?"

"I don't know, Papa. That's the way it works in the corporate world."

"Then something is wrong, beta. You need to be better than this. You went to IIM, you scored well, you are such an intelligent boy. You deserve more, beta."

"How I wish, Papa."

"*Ab mohalle walo ko kya batayenge?*" his mother's focus has clearly shifted.

"*Bol denge bahot achcha kam kiya isliye company ne chhutti pe bheja hai. Company ne paise bhar ke Ladakh bheja, aur to aur ye bhi bola ki thoda aram karo, bahot kam kar liya.*"

Sid rolls his eyes. This was the exact reason he is living away from Lucknow and their own clan in general. His parents have always wanted Sid to be seen as the achiever in their clan and they don't mind telling white lies to uphold that position. Sid is of the opinion that "Why is Sid home?" is not a question they should entertain from neighbors, and if they do, then they should be honest. But he knows his parents are set in their way of life and they are not going to listen to him. So he decides to ignore it. He has bigger things to worry about.

Although he defends himself in front of his father, he starts thinking about his position in the company. What his father said is absolutely true. He doesn't deserve to be treated like this. He nurtured the company and performed well and despite that, he was unceremoniously thrown out. Maybe he missed a trick or two.

Maybe he should have done something to secure his position or maybe he should have done something to ensure whoever is behind his removal didn't succeed. He doesn't know what he could have done differently but he knows that he has to do something.

For now, he decides to take it easy. He sleeps without setting an alarm, wakes up whenever he feels like it. He asks his mother to make his favorite breakfast—*kachori, jalebis* or whatever he fancied at that time. Then he watches a movie, has lunch, and takes a nap in the afternoon.

In the evening, he has some tea with homemade snacks and then leaves to catch up with his long-lost friends or goes for a walk with his father, or simply hangs out and chats with his mother. After that, he accompanies his mother as she watches her regular TV shows, amusing himself by observing her enthusiasm and involvement in the on-screen *saas-bahu* rivalries.

After about a week, he prints all the nice pictures of his Ladakh trip. He, then, starts writing a long letter to Anjali. He just describes what he saw, peppers it with the pictures, some stickers, and glitter. He writes about 15 pages over the next 3–4 days and sends it to Anjali by post. He really feels happy after that.

He follows this relaxed lifestyle for the next few months. Usually, whenever he used to come home from Bangalore, his visits were fraught with conflict because he kept trying to challenge the ways of his parents. He would try to teach them Internet banking or how to use an ATM card, thinking that this would make their lives easier, not understanding why they would constantly resist. They didn't want to change. He would also suggest some modifications or renovations to the house and they would not agree. They would say that they were happy with the way their house was.

Sid would feel irritated and argue or sometimes he would give up resentfully. This time things were different. He doesn't know how long he is going to stay with them, since he wants to stay till he figures things out. He doesn't know when that would be. So he decides to live and let live, accepts their way of life and tries to live it their way. Suddenly, a whole new world opens up to him about his parents and their lifestyle.

When he goes with his father to the bank to fill in the passbook, he realizes that what he used to consider as useless activity is actually a social activity for his father. Filling up the passbook is just an excuse. He sees his friends in the bank who have also come there to fill in their passbooks, the bank employees know his father and they exchange pleasantries—they ask about their health, how their kids are doing, what are their Diwali plans, etc.

The passbook is filled in five minutes, but his father easily spends an hour in the bank. Sid realizes one hard fact about old age. One needs to find activities to be done on a daily basis to occupy the time. Old couples like Sid's parents who don't live with their children have to fight a constant battle to drive away boredom. They may have enough money and their health may also be reasonably good, but filling in each day is a big challenge.

So they don't take to Internet banking. Efficiency is not the main focus for them anymore. Along with Internet banking, Sid discovers many other aspects of their life that are designed to fight boredom and fill up their time with mundane but fulfilling activities.

Sid sees another example of this when he goes vegetable shopping with his mother. In the past, he had contacted a vegetable vendor who could deliver chopped vegetables to their doorstep every day. *What can be better than that?* He had thought to himself, only to realize that his mother wasn't interested in it. For her, buying vegetables was an excuse to step out of the house, kill some time, and of course, derive pleasure from a shopping activity.

Earlier, when his mother would haggle with the vegetable and fruit vendors, Sid would say, "It's okay, Ma. We have money, they don't. It's okay if we pay a little bit extra." But his mother would never agree. Instead, she would ask him not to come with her when she went vegetable shopping. This time, Sid decides not to stop his mother from haggling. In fact, he haggles right alongside her and relishes the smile on her face. Him accepting her lifestyle makes her very happy.

She also takes Sid to the *chakki* to get freshly ground *atta*. Sid no longer complains and cheerily accompanies her. Her happiness knows no bounds.

For Sid's family, this is the best period of their life. They have their beloved son living with them and he is doing whatever they want. Of course, the question of marriage lingers in the background, but Sid has made it clear he is not ready for that. Sid is also feeling happy with this arrangement. Living away from his parents always makes him feel guilty, like he is not being useful or cannot share their burdens. Over these past few months, he feels as if some void inside him has been filled. He feels calm, content, and relaxed.

Of course, he is still unsure of what his next steps are. His removal from Creativity Unlimited is nothing short of a devastating breakup. He is still finding it difficult to accept and needs to heal before he can decide what to do. Staying with his parents and following their lifestyle and gaining their approval turns out to be the perfect healing process. He is quite sure that he doesn't want to join any competitor.

For starters, he would not enjoy working in their culture and secondly, he still couldn't come to terms with doing something that is against the interest of Creativity Unlimited. After all, it is like his first love, perhaps more than that, because he chose the company over his first love—Anjali. One good thing is, he doesn't really need to do anything to earn money. He has enough equity and savings and is free to do what he wants to.

So to heal faster, he has shut himself from Creativity Unlimited. He is deliberately avoiding business newspapers and channels where he may accidentally hear about them. He has also requested all buddies not to call or contact him. He genuinely thinks that talking to buddies would be interference in their working with new bosses, which he has no interest in doing.

One day, Sid gets an invitation from a local MBA college to give a short speech at their career fair. Sid goes and speaks about his experience with entrepreneurship. The students love his speech. A few of them are so motivated that they decide to start their own company. The teachers in that college get a completely different perspective. They request Sid to be a guest lecturer in their college. Sid loves that idea. He loves staying home with his parents but he also needs to fill in his time.

He starts teaching at the local college. He loves the interaction with the younger generation. Although the students are just ten or fifteen years younger to him, it feels like they belong to a whole other world. Their thought process, ideas, and viewpoints;

everything is so different. Sid enjoys this. Mingling with younger kids makes him feel younger. Quickly, he becomes the coolest and most popular teacher in that college. Since he is not a full-time teacher, he has relaxed rules.

Sid's out-of-box methods get a new lease of life here. He doesn't restrict his teaching to classrooms. For instance, to teach the students negotiation skills, he asks them to purchase some vegetables from a bigger mandi and actually sell these by pushing carts in the neighborhood. To teach them leadership skills, he divides them into multiple groups and asks them to choose their leader and accomplish some complicated tasks. To teach them about advertising, he asks them to prepare an advertisement for unknown products and test them out with their parents.

These are all real-world learnings he has gained by running Creativity Unlimited and he enjoys passing them onto his students. It gives him an immense sense of fulfillment.

Time heals everything. Slowly, Sid gets so engrossed in this new phase of his life that he realizes that he is moving on. There are days when he no longer thinks of his life at Creativity Unlimited. However, he also realizes that not a day passes that he doesn't think about Anjali. She has still not replied to his letter.

As he is getting his priorities right, he realizes that letting her go was the biggest mistake of his life. She is perfect for him. Other people seemed to have realized this before him, because back in college, they used to be known affectionately as the 'old married couple.' He realized that till this idea of Creativity Unlimited entered, his mind was completely occupied by Anjali. He makes up his mind to win her back. He doesn't know when or how, but he was going to do it.

Time passes, and Sid gets used to the relaxed lifestyle of Lucknow. He has forgotten all about idly-dosas and relishes *paneer* and *chhole* cooked by his mother. He has forgotten all about internet banking and is helping his father fill up passbooks. He has forgotten all about his buddies and is enjoying with his students.

His evenings are not lonely anymore, he has his school friends to hang out with. Within just a span of a few months, his life has done a complete 180.

Sid thinks he has left Creativity Unlimited far behind in his life and he would never have to turn back. Although he is not sure where he is headed, he is sure that he will figure it out.

One relaxed afternoon, he is enjoying hot tea and homemade *mathari* with his parents, when his phone rings. It's Jo calling from Bangalore.

CHAPTER 15

The Mysterious Smile

Patience yields the broadest smiles.

Sid is startled to see the call. It is the last thing he expected. His lifestyle in Lucknow has evolved without social media. He has cut himself off from the world he belonged to.

But Jo calling him is something he can't ignore. Obviously, she needs help and would not have contacted him unless she was desperate. Her name does bring a smile to his face.

"Hey, dude, what's up?" Sid says.

"Hey, Sid. We are screwed, man!" His smile quickly fades.

"What happened? Are you okay?"

"Yes, I am fine but our company, your baby, is in big trouble."

"Calm down. Take a step back. This could be an overreaction."

"No, dude. Everything has gone upside down and if you don't do something, we will wind up on the streets in no time."

"Wow, is it that serious? Okay, tell me everything. Do you want me to call you back?"

"Yes, please. My balance is running out. It would be good if you can call."

Sid calls her back. Jo speaks nonstop for forty-five minutes. With each sentence, Sid gets a little more furious. He can't believe the extent to which Paul and Praveen have messed up the company that took him seven to eight years to build, in just seven to eight months.

"Jo, are you sure Praveen had a 'secret' agreement with Ramaiah? It seems very unlikely to me." His voice cannot hide the incredulous tone.

"Yes, dude! Ram-dude showed us a copy. It's signed by Pee-dude. Basically, we had prepared a campaign as per Praveen's instructions. We presented it to Ram. He didn't like it and he threw us out. But after a few days, Praveen asked us to release the same campaign to the media. He said Ramaiah approved it. We came up with the biggest media plan ever and ran the campaign.

"Initially, we were going with a normal schedule but Pee-dude asked us to increase the frequency. He kept meeting Ramaiah by himself. Every time he would come back from the meeting, he would seem very upset. He kept saying the approval rating has to go up, etc. We kept increasing the frequency but nothing much changed."

"Then?"

"Last week, he had a meeting with Ramaiah. I don't think the meeting went well because Pee was very upset when he came back. He asked us to stop the campaign completely. When we asked why, he said because it hasn't worked well. Bazinga! We knew that from the beginning. When we told him he was so upset, he yelled at Jee and me, *yaar*! And threw us out of your office."

Jo was sobbing. His heart broke for her, but a part of him was still amused that she still referred to it as 'his office'.

"It's okay, take another deep breath, keep going. Tell me everything."

"Then he went off to see Paul in that dingy club of his. After that, we saw very little of him in the office."

"He resigned?"

"No clue, man! We are not even sure where he is. But the bigger problem is that we have now started getting invoices from all the media houses for these stupid LTR campaigns. So I raised an invoice to LTR. As soon as I sent the first invoice, Ram-dude called me to their office and showed me the secret agreement Praveen had signed with him."

"What does that agreement say exactly?"

"Dude, I have never seen anything like it. It says unless the approval rating goes up by 15% in three months, LTR won't pay for the campaign. The cost has to be borne by Creativity Unlimited."

"That's crazy. Who the heck does that?"

"Traitors like Praveen. So we are getting all the invoices and we can't invoice anyone."

"Man! We are sandwiched." Sid could not help getting drawn into the situation. After all, it was—as she called it—'his baby'.

"As soon as we went to LTR, all our clients had sent us a termination notice. Praveen had said that he would win back LTR and everything would be okay. Now we have a triple whammy. Our usual clients are gone. LTR is gone and we have big fat bills to pay."

"That's a terrible situation to be in," Sid says. "What is Paul up to? Does he have any ideas?"

"Don't even ask. He is running like a headless chicken. He has no clue what should be done. We often hear about big fights he has with Praveen but I don't think both of them can solve this."

"Are you sure?"

"Very sure. We need you back, Sid. It is not just a company, it's your baby. It's our lifeblood. You need to come and set things right. You have to."

"It is not that simple, Jo. I was thrown out of the company. Unless Paul calls me or something, I cannot come back in, it's too hard."

"No, dude! Don't say that. Forget about the stakes and stuff. You have literally created this beautiful thing, can you see it go down the drain?" Jo was clearly emotional. Sid paused. Clearly, just saying 'no' was not working. Of course he was furious at what was happening, but he was also equally lost at what he could do.

"Jo, let me see what I can do."

"No, Sid. You have to do it. You have to get us out of this."

"I will try. Let me think. You take care. I will call you again."

He obviously does not want to commit to anything. He is not sure whether Paul and Praveen will allow him to do anything at all, much less save the company. Many things had to fall into place before Sid can get back into Creativity Unlimited.

Birbal Returns

In a feat of anger Akbar had banished Birbal from his kingdom and appointed another Diwan to run the show. But he soon realized his mistake. He realized that nobody could do that job better than Birbal himself.

In the meanwhile, Birbal was living in a far off city as a common man. But his intelligence and wit still shone through and he became the trusted confidant of the leader of that region, also known as a 'Patel'. He had disguised himself, so nobody knew who he was.

Akbar missed him terribly and wanted to ask him to come back, but he did not know how to find him in a kingdom as vast as his, especially since Birbal had hidden his true identity. Then Akbar thought of a plan.

He announced throughout his kingdom that he is calling for a gathering of wells in the kingdom. All the Patels were told to carry their wells and come to the royal palace. Obviously all other Patels except for the village where Birbal was staying, had no idea what to do. Birbal shared a witty idea with Patel.

Next day, Patel traveled to Delhi to see the king. When they met, he said, "We have gotten the wells to Delhi, but they are expecting a traditional welcome from the host. So the Badshah should send all the wells in Delhi over to us for a warm welcome."

Akbar smiled. He had found Birbal. He wasted no time in extending a ceremonial welcome for his trusted advisor.

After reading this story, Sid smiles, and decides to be patient. He reckons that although Paul is not as smart as Akbar, he still has some common business sense remaining that would push him to reach out to Sid; even if indirectly.

Fortunately, his patience pays off. In a few weeks, there is a full-page recruitment advertisement in *The Times of India.*

Creativity Unlimited, India's no. 1 digital advertising agency.

Looking for a new CEO.

Sid goes through the advertisement and smiles. It is tailor-made to fit Sid's profile, Paul's way of asking Sid to come back. Sid decides not to waste any more time.

He picks up his phone and calls Paul.

"Hi, Paul. How are things?" Sid asks.

"Sid, things are going from bad to worse, man." The relief in Paul's voice is almost audible, he speaks honestly.

"Yeah, I heard a few things from Jo last night."

"No, she doesn't know everything. It's far worse than that."

"What happened now?"

"Praveen resigned. He said he can't help any further!"

"How bad is it?"

"Very bad. If we don't do something, we will fold up in another six months."

After a long pause, Sid says, "I'll be there."

Sid feels as if he is coming out of hibernation. He enjoyed it but his life was calling him.

Before he leaves, he doesn't forget to drop a message to Anjali.

CHAPTER 16

Fight for Survival

The best defense is a good offense.

S id walks into the office. He is greeted with a loud cheer and thundering claps. Jo, Jee, and a few others sprint over and hug the breath out of him. He looks around the office. He feels like he cannot even see it. When he left, it was a vibrant place oozing with confidence. Now it looks like a gloomy, soul-sucking vacuum with all the cubicles and dull gray interiors, everything he fought against. This is accentuated with the faces all around him—the slouching shoulders, sad eyes and faces without a smile. He is still not sure what he can do but he vows to bring the smile back on their faces.

He walks into his cabin after about a year. He can't help feeling at home. There is a small void inside of him that is filled. He cannot ruminate on this for long, as Paul walks in. They exchange awkward smiles and half-hearted handshakes. They don't know how to start. Sid takes charge.

"When did you know about the secret agreement?" Sid asks.

"A few days ago when the finance department told me that LTR is not accepting invoices," says Paul.

"Did you ask Praveen about it?"

"Of course. Initially, he feigned ignorance. So I asked him to go to LTR and sort it out. Then he started giving excuses about why he can't go."

"Then?"

"I asked Jo and Jee to go. They came back and told me that they saw the agreement. Still, I didn't believe it. I thought Jo has an axe to grind so she is trying to trap Praveen."

"No, she would never do such a thing."

"Yeah. That's when she showed me pictures of the agreement. She is a clever girl. When she had the agreement in hand, she started praising the filter coffee. So they got distracted, that's when she took pictures of the agreement and showed it to me."

"That's more like Jo," Sid says with a smile.

"I showed the pictures to Praveen. That's when he resigned. He is gone."

"Such unprofessional behaviour!" Sid says.

"I didn't expect it from him," Paul says. "But you know what is most ironic. He has sympathy from the media and the other companies. Everyone thinks we screwed up."

Sid smiles at the use of the word 'we'. But he is happy to hear it.

"What is the situation with our old clients?" Sid asks.

"A lot of them are gone. A few had longer notice periods; we are still working with them. Their retainers are keeping the home fires burning. Otherwise, we are in bad shape, Sid."

"How much is the media bill for LTR?"

"Massive. We can't afford it. I don't have that kind of money. We will have to close the company down if you can't find a way out of this."

Sid notices that 'we' has gradually turned into 'you'.

Paul says, "Sid, please do something to save this company. I know I wasn't nice to you. I got carried away with Praveen and threw you out. I am sorry. I shouldn't have done it. I shouldn't have trusted Praveen so much. You have built this company from scratch. You know how to manage it."

This is not a situation Sid knows how to manage. Would his trusted advisor bring a solution?

Birbal and Armor Test

Fearing war with the neighboring kingdom, Akbar wants to stock up the armor for his army. He asks Birbal to find a supplier and purchase some armors from them. Birbal finds a good supplier and purchases 1,000 armors from him. When the supplier's men are delivering armors as per usual routine, they are stopped by some ministers who are jealous of his success and want to get Birbal in trouble.

They take out the armor, keep it on the floor and attack it with a sword. The armor breaks into pieces. They report this to Akbar who is naturally very upset. He summons the armor supplier to the court the next day. The armor supplier is worried. He seeks Birbal's advice on how to deal with the situation.

"But why did your armor break into pieces? Was it bad quality?" Birbal queries.

"No," exclaims the supplier, "you put any armor on the floor and attack with the sword, it would break. That's not how it is supposed to be tested. An armor is supposed to be tested by putting it on."

Birbal thinks for a while and says, "Then that is precisely what you should do tomorrow."

The next day, the armor supplier reaches the court wearing the armor. He requests, "I would ask the mightiest warrior to run a sword on me now. If I survive, that means my armor is good quality. If the armor breaks, I would die anyway and that's the punishment I deserve."

Needless to say, he passes this test with flying colors and wins back the armor contract.

Sid keeps the book down contemplatively. So it is time for him to take the armor test. He has to wear the armor and throw himself at all the swordsmen and trust the armor to help him survive. He knows nobody else can do it. Motivation comes from various sources. But the motivation that comes from the feeling that only you can set things right, is unparalleled.

Sid rolls up his sleeves and dives into it.

First, he calls his old clients to see if he can win them back. That would restore some revenue streams and make it easy for them to pay the media bills. Perhaps, the bank would extend credit based on the contracts and that would ease the pressure. Sid could then build the business with all his old clients and set things right.

But it is not easy to talk to these old clients. Most of them refuse to talk to Sid. Clients like Orchid Advertising where Sid has a personal rapport, at least call him back. But it is more to connect with Sid personally than to give him the account back. He tries to persuade them to start working again but they say it's too late. They also mention that there are other smaller agencies similar to Creativity Unlimited who are much cheaper and are more innovative now, so the companies are hiring them instead. Some buddies from Creativity Unlimited have crossed over to the other side and are working with these smaller agencies. So winning back old clients is no longer an option.

News-hungry media in India have played their tricks. The murmurs about things going wrong in Creativity Unlimited have been amplified, with columns and columns written about how they have lost their mojo. Most of the media tried to contact Paul and Praveen to get their version of the story but both of them were too occupied to manage the media. As a result, most of the stories in the media are one-sided and sound like an obituary for Creativity Unlimited. New clients are naturally not going to be easy to get.

Sid, racking his brain, arrives at the only conclusion—winning back LTR is probably the only way out. He has to crack Ramaiah. He picks up the phone and asks the receptionist to book an appointment with Ramaiah.

Sid reaches Ramaiah's office. The staff offers the usual courtesies. Sid relishes the filter coffee. He is outwardly calm but frantically rehearsing his points in his mind. Ramaiah enters the room with folded hands and a smile.

"How are you, Siddhartha? I heard you took a break."

"Yes, I did. I had to clear my mind and get ready for new challenges," Sid says.

"Well, how can I help?"

It is not usual that Ramaiah starts to talk business so abruptly. It is a subtle hint to Sid that this may not be a very long meeting. Sid also realizes that if he is not able to crack Ramaiah now, then probably he will never be able to see him again. This meeting holds the key to the revival of Creativity Unlimited.

"As you are aware, Praveen has moved on."

"Yes. I am aware Praveen is no longer with you. In fact, he called me the other day and mentioned how things went from bad to worse."

So Praveen has played his cards.

"The thing is we are very keen to work with you and help you achieve your goals. But you would have to give us another chance."

Ramaiah leans back on his chair and says, "Praveen said the same thing last time and I gave him a chance."

Sid says, "Yes, I am aware. We are confident that this time, we will be able to help you better."

Ramaiah is amused. "What makes you think that?"

Sid says, "I am confident about the team."

Ramaiah smirks. "Are you talking about the same team who doesn't know how to dress properly or comb their hair?"

Sid can take everything but anyone pointing fingers at his buddies. He is rather possessive about them.

"There is nothing wrong with them. A look or your hair does not define your abilities. This is just the way they are."

"That is why you are where you are." Ramaiah is getting vicious.

"Sir, this is about our abilities in the hands of a better leader. I am humbly requesting you to give me one more chance and I am confident I can help your brand get strong recognition with young customers, the thing that you have always wanted.cc

Sid is trying his best, but Ramaiah is not in a mood to let up.

"Why should I do that? After all, I did trust your company and gave you another chance but you wasted it. I also lost everything."

"No, Sir." Sid is trying his best to not to lose his cool. He can already feel the blood rushing through his veins. "With all due respect, it was Creativity Unlimited who paid the entire production cost and media bill. The campaign may not have made your brand popular among the younger generation, but it has certainly helped you with your existing customer base. If I am not mistaken, last quarter you had a growth of 4% over last year."

Ramaiah is taken aback. *How does Siddhartha know? Looks like he is keeping a track of things much better than I thought,* Ramaiah thinks to himself.

The truth is when Sid was sipping coffee before Ramaiah arrived, he looked around and saw some graphs displayed on the noticeboard that showed the overall sales numbers. Sid's keen eye caught all the details in a flash. He continues, "Sir, both of us know that my company is best placed to help you achieve the objective. I am sorry that things didn't turn out as expected the last time. My company tried to do something different which didn't work, but we paid for our mistakes. This time, I am leading this, and I am confident we can achieve the objective."

At this point, Sid gets up with folded hands and says, "Your decision today will decide whether my company lives or dies. I humbly request you to give us one more chance to survive."

Under the hood of a hard-nosed businessman, Ramaiah was a kind-hearted person. His heart melted.

"Okay. One more month. That's all I can give you. I have already started searching for other media companies to help me but that process will take about a month. I can allow you to work until then. If you succeed, I will work with you."

"Done, sir." A big burden is lifted off Sid's chest. He starts to breathe easy.

"I would like to see an increase of 15% in approval rating among the younger generation," Ramaiah puts forth his long pending demand. Emotions in the corporate world are short-lived.

"Mr Ramaiah, I will come back to you with a plan and then let's decide whether a 15% increase in approval rating is the right metric. Who knows, maybe we can do better than that."

Ramaiah smiles. He thinks, *This guy is better than I thought.*

"When do we see the plan?"

"Tomorrow? Same time?"

Both of them sense the urgency. The clock has started ticking.

As he steps out of Ramaiah's office, his phone rings. He knows it is Paul. He just picks up and says, "We got a month. Let us see what we can do." He hangs up and calls Jo. "It is action time. Nobody goes home for the next couple of days."

Jo says, "AWESOME! That's the way we love it!"

CHAPTER 17

Cracking the Case

Finding a needle in a haystack? Bring a magnet.

Jo, Jee, and Sid are sitting in the brainstorming area in his cabin. There are a few opened packets of LTR snacks lying on the table, with bowls filled with these snacks. The trio is staring at the packets and the bowl for the past thirty minutes and nobody has uttered a word. That is the way they have done it in Creativity Unlimited for years. The campaign has to start with the personal experience of the product. Unless they have their own perspective about the product, they can't create a campaign for it. This is a process Sid has hammered into their minds.

The challenge in this case however, is very different. Both Jo and Jee know about LTR products and they hate them. They think the snacks they sell are from the previous century, too traditional and remind them of their stringent upbringing. Now how does one create a good campaign around the product they hate? So they are staring at the laddoos, the *Mysore Pak*, the *Patra Vadi*, the *chiwda*, the murukku and the *Shankarpali* packets lying on the table feeling a little lost.

"The packaging looks too cluttered and has that old world feel." Jee breaks the silence with his attempt.

"Colors are boring," Jo adds with a nod.

"Guys, we have been through this. Give me something." Sid poses a challenge.

"I can't even look at it for too long without getting a headache," Jee says.

"Then don't look at it but give me ideas." Sid shows his irritation.

At that, Jo claps and says, "That is a brilliant idea, Sid! That is what we will do. Generate ideas by not looking at it."

"What do you mean?" Jee asks, looking as confused as Sid feels.

"Let's do a blind taste with some buddies with different brands and see what comes out of it."

Sid is not particularly inspired by this idea, but sees this as a ray of hope.

Soon, they have twelve blindfolded buddies brought into the room. They are asked to taste one snack each and give their approval rating. They are also asked questions about when and where they would consume the snack. They are also asked to guess the brand. Jo and Jee have fun guiding their blindfolded colleagues through the room holding their hands. They spend a good half an hour of activity and laughter rings through the gray walls.

Jee writes the results on the whiteboard. The approval ratings for most snacks are bad except for one—the murukku. So they start discussing the feedback. It is a deep-fried spiced besan snack, which is usually consumed along with afternoon tea. It is known for its spiral design and spiky texture. To their surprise, along with the highest rating, the murukku was the only snack for which no one could guess the brand. It also came up that this was a snack that could be eaten anytime. Jo's shot in the dark has worked well, they think.

They repeat the exercise with a few more blindfolded buddies and only with murukku. The results are consistent. The approval ratings are high. Nobody is able to guess which brand it is and they get more suggestions on where else this snack can be consumed. The one that clearly stands out is—'with my evening beer'.

This is totally unexpected. How could one imagine the traditional brand like LTR to be associated with beer and pubs?

Jee is ecstatic. Sid has a smile on his face but Jo is still looking for something more.

She brings all the buddies who have tasted the murukku back to the room. Now, they are not blindfolded. But they are shown products and asked for the rating. As soon as they see the product, they say, "Oh, it is murukku! Must be from LTR," and approval ratings also drop significantly.

Jee says, "It's puzzling, isn't it?"

Sid says, "They just hate the brand, right?"

Jo with a spark in his eyes, says, "They may hate the brand but love the product. Look at the approval ratings. They are near perfect."

Sid says, "True."

"Did you notice one more thing?" Jo asks.

"What?" Jee desperately wants to feel as positive as Jo.

"When did they guess the LTR brand?"

"As soon as we showed the product to them. Even before they tasted the snack."

"Exactly. The shape of murukku is so typical and LTR's name is strongly linked to that."

"Isn't that the problem?" Jee is still lost.

Jo says mockingly, "What has our great mentor Siddharth Sharma-baba taught us? Every problem is an . . . "

" . . . opportunity," both Jo and Jee say in a chorus.

Sid smiles. He is assured that he has brought in a real change in people around him.

"So let us start from the top. The only snack with a decent blind approval rating is murukku. It is not strongly associated with the LTR brand in the blind test. But as soon as they see the product, they know it's murukku from LTR and the approval ratings drop," Sid summarizes.

Jee is still unable to see how this is going to help.

"I still see this as a problem we can't overcome."

Sid looks at the watch. It is almost 8 p.m. He says, "Let us take our dinner break and meet again at 9:30, and look at it with a fresh mind."

"Okay. That sounds good."

Sid picks the phone and orders something. Jo and Jee step out. First they take their customary cigarette break, then they go to the nearby Darshini restaurant for a quick bite. Jo thinks the solution is staring at her in the face and she will get it if she is able to concentrate for a while. Jee, on the other hand, is quite confused and thinks there is no solution to this paradoxical situation. He reiterates all the arguments, all over again.

"People like their murukku when they don't know it is from LTR. As soon as they know it is from LTR, the approval rating drops. Now how can we use this situation to improve the brand approval rating for LTR?"

Jo says, "See this means that in this case, that is for this product among these customer-segments, that the product leads the brand. Correct?"

"Yes. Seems so customers are liking the product more than the brand."

"So if there is some way in which we can just present the product and not the brand, LTR will actually do better."

"Don't go and tell this to Ram-dude man! He will make you into a murukku," Jee says.

Both of them laugh.

"Ya, man! He is proud of his brand," Jo exclaims.

"And to real customers, how are you going to give the product without showing the brand? Even if you open the packet and give the murukku to the customers, they are going to guess that it is from LTR anyway," Jee continues. "So, unless you are able to hide both the brand name and shape of murukku, you can't fool the customer. The only solution I can think of is, keep the taste exactly the same but make the product and brand look like something else," Jee says with a laugh, thinking that he has cracked the biggest joke.

But Jo exclaims, "Wow! Jee, you are a genius."

"What did I do now?" Jee is puzzled.

"That is exactly what I like about you," Jo says as hugs him and starts blowing flying kisses toward him. "You are a genius and you have no idea."

"Now can you tell me what is happening here?"

This public display of affection scandalises patrons in the restaurant who cannot associate these actions with platonic relationships. Jo, as usual, doesn't care.

"Well, you just solved the problem. We need to present the murukku to the customers without making it look like a typical murukku and without putting it in LTR packaging. Then, the customers can shelve their biases away and enjoy the product!"

"But . . . how?" Jee is skeptical.

"I don't know. Now finish your coffee and let us go talk to Sid."

Sid is expecting the duo at 9:30, so naturally he is surprised to see them rushing in at 9:05. Obviously, they have something good to share. Jo rushes to his office, catches her breath and says, "We cracked it. I think there is a solution. I don't think it is easy, but if we can do it, I am confident we are through."

"Calm down. What is it?"

Jo has started taking big gulps from a water bottle so Jee starts to explain. "We think for this segment and for this product category, the LTR brand is a liability. Actually, it is the brand image and associations that are clouding the customers' mind and not allowing them to enjoy this product." By now Jee has gotten into the groove.

"So we have to present the murukku as something else and pack it in some other packaging and then get the customers to like it."

Sid hears this but he doesn't know if it is doable. How can he go and tell Ramaiah that his brand is a liability? He knows that for families that own such brands, the brand is like an offspring. They nurture it, take care of it and are also emotionally attached to it. They don't want to hear anything against the brand.

But based on the small experiment they did, what Jo and Jee are saying holds water. Besides, he doesn't have any other idea. So he decides to take this idea forward. He says, "Ok, assuming that we are able to convince Ramaiah about this idea, what will we do next. Suppose he says—Ok if not murukku, what would you like this product to be. A square, a rectangle or a hexagon?"

This is what Jo and Jee love about Sid. He is always one step ahead, forcing them to think harder.

"Well, why should it be any complicated geometrical shape. Why can't it be like a straight line," says Jo. She never liked maths and hates anything complicated.

"Ya, I like that! Like french fries!" Jee exclaims.

"Interesting. Young customers also have a natural affinity toward french fries, thanks to fast food," says Sid.

"So the moment it doesn't look like murukku, customers would invent newer occasions to eat it," says Jee.

The brainstorming has started to give way to concrete ideas.

"If it is not murukku, then what will we call it?" Sid asks.

Sid has always told them that in brainstorming sessions asking the right question is as important as coming up with a new idea. So Sid has resorted to the role of asking the right questions.

"I don't know, maybe Besan Fries or straight murukku," Jee blurts out.

Sid says, "No, guys, we have fooled the customer, right? The customer shouldn't be able to guess that this is murukku or anything to do with murukku. So no besan fries. That's a giveaway."

Jee says, "Of course, Sid. I was joking. I was having fun . . . do you know fun?"

Jo says, "Fun Fries. That's it. That is what we will call them."

Jee and Sid nod and say, "Yeah, that sounds nice."

"Now what about packaging? How can we hide the LTR brand?" Sid is persistent about asking the right questions.

"I think we should do a limited test launch before asking Ramaiah to invest in new packaging."

"Yeah, man! Otherwise, he will make an agreement and say you pay for it," Jo says sardonically.

They all laugh.

Jo says, "See? This is what we missed when you were away, Sid. We could never laugh in the office. Everyone was so serious. Right now, we are working late in the night but it seems like fun. Back then, it was all stress and pressure."

"I know. I also missed this," says Sid.

"Well, you're back now, so let's make the most of it!" Jee reconciles.

"We should do a test launch of 'Fun Fries' with the youth. I already love the name," says Jo.

"As per our study, the top occasion of usage of Fun Fries would be with an evening drink like a beer," says Jee.

Sid says, "That is great. We already know the pub owners. Let us do a short promotion with them on one of these weekends and see how it goes."

"But the big question is who will bell the cat?" Jo asks.

"Naturally, this is my responsibility," says Sid.

"Fair enough. What time do you have to visit Ramaiah tomorrow?" Jee gets down to business.

"We are going together. 9 a.m. please."

"Ok, Sid. You carry on home. Both of us will work on the presentation and make sure it's ready by tomorrow morning," Jo reassures Sid.

Sid says, "Sure, it sounds good. I think it would be midnight by the time you finish. You don't have to haggle with auto fellows. Maybe you can sleep here. Switch on the air conditioner."

Jo and Jee smile as they feel loved and cared for.

Who gets such a caring boss? They think to themselves.

"Yes, boss!" Jee says.

Sid drives home. Jo and Jee take a cigarette break and get down to work. They have a perfect understanding of each other. They divide the work amicably and start doing it with utmost sincerity. No cracking jokes, no social media, no distractions.

Sid wondered why others complain about the young generation. Excite them, challenge them, give them something they like and watch them flourish.

CHAPTER 18

Light at the End
of the Tunnel

Persistent efforts pave the way for tangible results.

The next day, Sid, Jo and Jee gather in Ramaiah's office. They are served the same filter coffee as per the standard routine. Jo and Jee ask for Coke. This time they are under no pressure to behave a certain way. They feel free and respected for the choices they make.

After some time, Ramaiah walks in. After short pleasantries, they get down to business.

Ramaiah asks, "So where is the campaign?"

Both Jo and Jee look at Sid.

"No, sir," Sid starts confidently. "We don't think we are ready for the campaign yet. Communication campaign is the last step. We have to ascertain a few important things before that."

Sid is taking his time to deliver the news. He wants to go as slow as possible. He is weighing every word.

"Such as?" Ramaiah bends down toward the desk but his right hand is still covering his mouth. Sid concludes that he has piqued his interest but he is not home yet.

"I would like to assess the approval rating of the product, the first and probably the most important P in the marketing mix."

"We have already done that and the approval rating is low, but there is nothing wrong with the product," Ramaiah states as a matter of fact.

"I agree. But most of the research we have done is the approval rating of brand and product combined, correct?"

"Yes, that is true."

"Before recommending how to improve the brand approval rating, I would like to study product approval rating and see if the brand approval rating is in fact suffering because of the product or vice versa."

"That is an interesting idea!" Ramaiah bends forward further and points his index finger at Sid in an appreciative way.

"Thank you, sir." Sid has always followed a principle—celebrating and acknowledging every small win.

Ramaiah looking at him with a smile was the biggest win in the last few days.

"How do you suggest we do that?" The idea looks like it is growing on Ramaiah.

"We did a small exercise at our office which gave us some pointers."

"What were the results?"

Jo opens her mouth to say something when Sid gestures to her that he will continue.

"It's too premature to share the findings but we definitely know what we want to do."

"Ok, what is it? Wait, let me call my assistant to take notes." Ramaiah seems quite happy.

"Can we have one more coffee please?" By now Sid knows how to please Ramaiah further.

"Of course." Ramaiah is always happy when someone appreciates their secret formula.

Coffee is served. In the meanwhile, Ramaiah's assistant scampers in with a notepad.

"We would like to have only murukku for our test. But we don't want it in the spiral shape that we usually get. For the testing, we need them like french fries. Four to six inches in length. No change in taste."

Ramaiah asks his assistant to check if that is feasible. The assistant scampers back out.

"What else do you need?"

"Can we get this in packaging that doesn't have the LTR brand name on it?"

"That is a strange request."

"Yes, sir. We understand, but for our project to be successful we need it in the non-branded pack."

"Let me check that too. But now I definitely want to know what you are planning to do."

"Well, sir, before we come up with the campaign we would like to understand how customers consume your products. So we would sample some of the products to customers and see if they like it."

"So you are going to give it away for free?"

"That we haven't decided yet."

"There is no way I am going to distribute my precious murukku for free to these young guns."

"You don't have to, sir. Let us go step by step. Let us first decide whether we are able to get these in the non-branded pack first."

They wait for a couple of minutes. The assistant comes in.

"I checked with the General Manager. He said he will have to modify the nozzle and platform. He will stop it from revolving and that would make the murukku in a straight line like they want."

"That's good. They are asking for non-branded packaging, do we have anything?"

"Yes, sir. Three years back, we tried to change the packaging. But you didn't like the color. So I cancelled the order. But they refuse to refund our deposit. So you ask them to supply the packaging material equivalent to that amount. That packaging doesn't have the LTR logo because we took it out from the second print run."

"Fantastic. I always knew that packaging would be useful somewhere."

"But there is one thing the GM said, sir."

"What is it?" Ramaiah asks.

"If they make us do all these changes, the minimum quantity they need to take is one ton," said the assistant.

"That's too much," blurts out Jee.

Sid shoots him a look. The discussion needs to go smoothly. He still hasn't planned what he will do with these products. He is just happy to get them. Luckily, Ramaiah doesn't seem to have heard Jee.

"So, Siddharth, you will get what you wanted. But I can't give you one-ton murukku for free. You have to bear the cost price. My assistant will mail you the invoice."

"But, sir, we are already paying for the advertisement. How can we pay for one ton of murukku? It is quite hard for us," Sid says.

"Nothing comes easy, young man. If you want it, these are my conditions," Ramaiah says, the tone of finality ringing loud in his voice. He has bought into the idea but like the true businessman that he is, he is not ready to commit any financial resources for Creativity Unlimited. Trust is like a glass vessel. Once it breaks, you can stick it back together but the cracks always remain like a webbed reminder.

"Ok, sir. Let us meet tomorrow again where we will present you with the plan about what we will do with this one-ton murukku."

"Sure. I look forward." Ramaiah gets up with folded hands.

Back in the office, Jo, Jee, and Sid are again in the brainstorming area, wondering how they can use one ton of murukku. It is quite literally a big problem. But like Sid always says, it is also a big opportunity. They now had to figure out how to tap it.

"One ton means how much, yaar?" Jo asks a basic question to get her math right.

"It is 1,000 kilograms. It is huge! Like . . . the size of a polar bear! What are we going to do with so much murukku?" Jee sounds desperate.

"Let us break it down. 1,000 kilograms means one million grams. So if one customer eats 100g, we need one lakh such customers to finish one ton. Is that right?" Jo asks.

"Correct!" Jee says.

"Where are we going to get all these customers?" Jo asks.

Jee is extremely irritated. He says, "I feel Ramaiah is a crook. Instead of paying us money as an agency, he is making us pay. He tricked Pee-dude into paying his advertisement bill. Now he is palming off one ton of his shitty murukku."

Jo is still committed to the cause. She says, "He is not palming off. He is giving it to us for sampling."

Jee says, "No, dude. If it was given for sampling, he would pay for it. But he is expecting money from it. So do you realize what he is doing?"

"What?"

Jee says, "He is selling us one ton of his murukku, dumbo. That's it. If we decide to take this sampling thing forward, which I think we shouldn't, we have to pay another big chunk to LTR."

Jo says, "I don't necessarily see it that way."

Jee says, "I clearly see us standing on the road-side and selling murukku for R-dude."

Jo says, "Stop. Don't be ridiculous."

Sid steps in. "Guys, don't fight. I don't think we have a way out here. We have to somehow do it. Every problem is an opportunity for innovators like us, right? Think what we can do?"

Jee says, "I know what I can do. I can go for a cigarette break."

Jo says, "I was about to suggest that."

Jee asks, "Don't you want to join?"

Jo grins and says, "Nopes. I want to give company to my boss."

Jee is further irritated and storms off.

Sid says, "Let us start from the beginning and state all questions we want answers to."

Jo goes to the board and writes, "We need to find one lakh customers who would buy the murukku."

"No, Jo. You have combined many problems together. Write one problem in each line."

As Jo starts to write, Sid says excitedly, "Wait a second. Who said we want one lakh customers?"

"Jee said. You know I am weak in math."

"If we get one ton of murukku, which means 1,000 kilograms and every customer eats 100 grams, then we need only 10,000 customers. That is not too difficult to get."

Jo says, "Really? Are you sure?" While saying this, she pulls out her calculator and says, "Oh damn, you are right, Sid. It is indeed, 10,000. That is not too bad."

Right then, Jee walks back.

Jo says to him mockingly, "We solved the problem you had created. We need only 10,000 customers now."

Jee says sheepishly, "Yeah, I realized I made a calculation mistake as soon as I took my second puff. So I ran back."

Jo writes on the board now.

1. Find 10,000 customers.

2. Make them pay for 100g murukku each.

Jee says, "No, not murukku. Fun Fries."

Jo amends her words.

Sid says, "So far we have done sampling exercises. We give a sample of the product to the customer and ask him how he or she likes it and what was preferred."

Jo also adds, "And we also ask them what price they would be ready to pay for it?"

Jee says, "How will that work now? We just need to make them pay. It's bound to fail."

Jo says, "Jee . . . you don't know but you are brilliant. You have a solution to every problem. Just that you don't know."

Jee says, "No hugging, please. Tell me how did I solve this problem?"

Jo says, "This is what we will do. We will give a sample to the customer for the first time, and if they want one more helping, they need to buy. Simple."

Jee says, "But why will they buy? There are so many snacks they can choose from. Who will buy the new stuff?"

Jo says, "That is exactly what we have to find out. Who is paying for this new stuff? Some of them will, some of them won't. So we will have a clear idea of who the customer segment is, we will have a clear idea whether they prefer the product and most importantly, we will know what price they are willing to pay because they will have to pay it."

Sid says, "Bingo! That is what we will do. In my management course, we had studied this technique but never used it. It's called a virtual marketplace."

"Ok. Let's do it." Finally, Jee is on board.

Jo says, "Sid, now I think we can handle this. If you want to step out, it is fine."

"I definitely want to step out and I want to play the final act in the resurrection of my company."

Jee is surprised, "And what would that be?"

Sid sounds mysterious. "You will know. Just do me a favor. Don't talk to anyone that we are about to crack LTR ok?"

Jee and Jo say in a chorus, "You got it!"

CHAPTER 19

Staking Claim

Having nothing to lose puts you in the best position.

Sid steps out and calls Paul.

"I would like to see you, Paul."

"Now? Is it urgent?" Paul asks.

"Yes, it is. It is about LTR."

"Okay. Let us meet at UB Plaza in thirty minutes."

When Sid reaches, Paul is already there, which is quite rare.

"What is the news, Sid? Will we make it?"

"Not sure, Paul. We are trying our best. We had a couple of meetings with Ramaiah, which seem okay, but Ramaiah is a shrewd businessman."

"What is he saying?" Paul asks impatiently. "Is he waiving off the advertisement bill?"

Paul is a true-blue investor, focused on money all the time.

"Not even close. In fact, if we want to resurrect the account, we need to invest more."

"I am sick of this. I don't think I can invest any more in Creativity Unlimited."

"Can't you? Then how do we come out of it, Paul?"

"I am not sure. I am running out of ideas and more importantly, running out of patience."

Sid also has a worried face but deep inside he is happy. The discussions are progressing along the lines that he wanted.

"It has been a rough ride for one year, right?"

"You bet, man. I shouldn't have listened to that bloody Praveen. Everything was going smoothly until he stepped in."

"I know." Sid wanted Paul to brood a bit more.

"I didn't have to come to the office. I could celebrate my Onam and Vishu in Kerala. Go to Munnar whenever I want."

"I know and I like your farmhouse, too."

"That is my most favorite place in the world. Overlooking tea estates, on my small hill. Sip fresh tea, read the newspaper, eat paratha. That is life, Sid, that is life. I don't like Bangalore. Life here is full of hassle."

"I know. You shouldn't have to work hard at this age."

"Exactly. I had already retired eight years back. This Praveen came and made me work again."

"I think you deserve better."

"Yes. But what to do? The bad news is not ending."

"I think I can do something to solve this issue."

"Can you?" Paul was delighted. "How will you do that, Sid?"

"Right now, we are in a hopeless situation, right?"

"Right."

"We need investment, but you don't want to invest anymore, right?"

"Right"

"If we fail to regain LTR, then we are as good as dead, right?"

"Right."

"And chances of getting back LTR are reducing by the day, right?"

"Right."

"So let me buy over this company from you at this stage. I want to increase my stake from the current 25% to 100%."

"Are you sure, Sid? Because if the company folds, you will get 99% of 0, which is still zero."

"Yes, I am sure. I should have done it long ago. But better late than never."

Paul asks, "But how much will you pay for additional equity?"

Sid says, "Well, that is what we should discuss. I have two options. I can either pay you a large sum now and buy over your equity or promise you a fixed monthly Director's remuneration irrespective of what happens to the company."

For the first time, Paul is hearing something that he never anticipated. He says, "What is your preferred option?"

However, the discussion is going exactly how Sid wants. He says, "The second option, of course. I don't have money to give you for the first option at all. I have to borrow it from the market. At this stage, it is not just difficult, it is distracting. I would prefer to pay you a fixed amount monthly for the next twenty years even if it costs me a lot more."

"But why do you want to do that?"

"Paul, this is not just a company for me. This is my life. When I was away for almost a year, I realized how much this means to me. I don't want to lose this again."

"It will never happen again. You have my word."

"It is ok, Paul. Let us make it formal. Let us not go by promises and emotions now."

Paul says, "If I get five lakh rupees a month for the rest of my life, and if I don't have to bother about ups and downs, then I am ready to increase your stake to 100%."

"Done."

"Are you sure, Sid? I will put a contract in place for this. If you can't pay, you will go to jail."

"I am sure, Paul. The time away from all this was no different than being in jail."

"But right now, the company doesn't generate anywhere close to this."

"It is my problem, Paul. Make a contract, I will sign it."

Sid gets up and goes to the counter to pay the bill.

Paul is left dumbstruck.

A year away from Creativity Unlimited has made Sid wiser and more focused on protecting what he loves the most. Whenever they met in the past, it was always Paul who paid the bill. But today, Sid takes the initiative and pays the bill before Paul can realize what hit him. Paul thinks to himself that actually he should be happy. Sid has agreed to his conditions.

If he got Rs. 5 lakh per month for the rest of his life and he never has to work again, he would be the happiest person on the Earth. But he is unable to figure out how Sid is going to do it. That makes him feel as if he has lost the negotiation. But now he can't change it.

Sid pays the bill and comes back to Paul and says, "I have just one condition that we should sign this document today. I want everything to be done and dusted today itself."

Paul says, "What is the hurry?"

"Well, that is my condition. If you don't do it, then you are the one holding 75% of zero."

"Right."

"And both of us don't want it, right?"

"Right."

"So should I come to the Cosmopolitan Club at 6 p.m.?"

"Yes."

Sid leaves. Paul is almost hypnotized. He can't feel anything. Although he got precisely what he wants, he feels as if he has lost out something big. But now the moment has passed, he can't reverse it. He thinks, *Maybe I should have asked for more, maybe I should have asked what Sid is up to, perhaps I should have asked how he is going to do it.*

All these thoughts stress him out. He decides to forget about it and dials his lawyer's phone number.

Sid can't believe what just happened. He doesn't know if he committed too much to Paul. But he is happy to get complete control of Creativity Unlimited. He thinks to himself, *I will figure out how to pay him that money, but let me have my company for myself. I should have done it long back but better late than never.*

He feels as if a significant burden is lifted off his chest. That is when he thinks of Anjali.

An hour back, Creativity Unlimited was not mine but I dared to speak my mind out and I got the whole company for myself. Maybe I should do the same for Anjali. She has moved on, I haven't. I still love her so she deserves to know, Sid thinks to himself.

He pulls out his phone and this time he places a video call to Anjali. This time, she picks immediately. In past few calls, there is always an awkward silence in the beginning but not this time.

Without pausing, Sid blurts out exactly what his heart feels. "Anjali, I love you. You are the only love of my life."

Anjali says, "Sid, stop. When we met last time, I told you I am over this. I told you I am seeing someone, right?"

Sid says, "Yes, you did. But that makes no difference to me, I still love you."

Anjali looks a little taken aback. "Aren't you angry with me that I dumped you?"

Sid says, "No. Not at all. It has made no difference to my feelings for you. I probably deserved it, the way I treated you. To love me or not is your choice. I just want you to know I love you no matter what."

Anjali says, "Sid, stop. Don't confuse me."

Sid says, "No, I am not. I am not even asking you to change anything or to love me or to marry me. I just want to tell you that I love you and just want you to be happy. That's all."

And he hangs up.

He feels ecstatic.

Sid reaches back to the office. Jo and Jee are in Sid's cabin, busy working on the project. Jee is making calls to the pubs, to finalize the promotion date and time. Jo is busy analyzing the prices of snacks available at the pubs to accurately price the Fun Fries.

Sid asks, "How are we doing, guys?"

Jo says, "Umm . . . I am still analysing the data on how the snacks are priced at these pubs. Once I know the price point, I will also analyze the typical quantity of snacks consumed by each patron. Then we will know roughly how many patrons we need and we will crunch the numbers to see how many pubs we need to get into."

Sid says, "That's great."

Jee says, "Dude, most of the pubs are pushing back. They are so used to a sampling exercise that is free that they are unable to understand what we are trying to do."

Sid says, "Can you tell me again what you have told them?"

Jee says, "I mentioned that we would give them the sampling of the Fun Fries but the customers have to purchase them at a price we mention. So, most of them are skeptical and are saying that this will not work. They are saying that for a new product, nobody wants to pay anything."

Sid says, "Their concerns are valid. We must address them."

Jee says, "But how? We have to sell one-ton murukku right? We can't give it for free. I wish we had some magic by which they get so hooked on to it that they are ready to pay for more."

"That's a brilliant idea," shouts Jo. From where she is sitting across the table, she starts blowing kisses.

Jee is irritated again. He says, "Stop that! What did I do now?"

"You dumb, dumb genius! You solved the problem again and you are so cute that you still don't know about it."

"Okay, tell me already!"

Sid is also a bit confused; he says, "Jo, I would like to hear it, too."

Jo says, "We will give some initial quantity as a free sample. Then, if they get hooked on it, we ask them to pay for the rest. It's a 'virtual marketplace', remember? We have to coexist with other snacks. We need to see whether they get hooked on this. We can also judge what price they are willing to pay for this."

Sid is elated. "That is a brilliant idea, Jo."

Jee says, "If we do that, we can promise a handsome margin to pubs, too. I am sure they will take it with both hands."

Jo says, "Great. Please check with them what their expected margin is and I will build it into the cost."

Jee says, "This is exciting. It would be like an actual launch, just that we will watch how each pub is doing on an hourly basis."

Jo says, "Ok, let me get cracking on the price and quantity."

Jee says, "I will find out as many pubs who are willing to support us as I can."

Both of them get back to their work. Sid feels that he is blessed to have such coworkers. They are so driven and self-motivated. They can define the problem, complement each other to find a solution, and without worrying about their boss' approval, they feel empowered enough to go ahead and implement them. He knows he has made the right decision by asking Paul to give him a 90% stake, what he has to pay to get it is inconsequential.

That is when he realizes that there is one more loose end he needs to tie. He picks up the phone and asks the receptionist to get the earliest possible appointment for Mr Ramaiah.

Sid is nervously sitting in Ramaiah's cabin. He has finished his filter coffee and is waiting for him to arrive. In the morning, he negotiated with Paul successfully. Will he be the second time on the same day? Sid's mother always believed in daily fortune. She would always say, "If your stars are aligned on that day, anything can happen."

Sid never believed in the fortune-tellers and astronomy. But today he wishes that it is accurate and hopes that his stars are aligned. Just then, Ramaiah walks in. Sid stands up to greet him. Both of them greet each other with folded hands.

"Yes, tell me, Siddharth, what brings you here?"

"Sir, as you know our company is in a spot of trouble because of recent developments. We decided to work with you and we lost most of our clients. They were ad agencies who thought that we shouldn't be dealing directly with companies like you and compete with them."

"Yes, I read about that in the newspapers."

"It would have worked very well, if our engagement was successful and we got your contract."

"Correct. But what happened was not our fault," says Ramaiah warily.

"Yes, agreed. I am not here to blame anyone. I am merely stating the facts. I am not drawing any conclusions or assigning reasons."

"Ok, go on," says Ramaiah.

"Instead of a successful engagement, our company now has to pay for a huge failed ad campaign."

"Hmm."

"I was hoping to come out of this situation but now we have to purchase one ton of murukku from you to prove that we can do it."

"Ah, hm."

"Sir, with due respect, this is the last gamble we can play. This is the last risk we can take. This is the last straw that is going to break the camel's back."

Sid takes a pause. The pause makes Ramaiah feel uneasy, which is precisely what Sid wants.

"Sir, you are a great human being. You are so successful, yet so humble. You always take care of people around you and ensure they are well off. I know everything about how your father and you have built this company bit by bit, and how you have taken care of your own people."

"That is right."

"Sir, if we are successful in this test marketing, then I want this to be the last test my company has to go through. I am confident we will be able to take your brand to young customers. I am sure we will be able to help you achieve your objectives but unfortunately, my company can't take any more risks."

"What campaign have you planned for now?"

Sid says, "Sir, it is a very unconventional campaign, perhaps such a marketing campaign has never happened in India before. But we are confident that this is going to work."

"What if it doesn't?" Ramaiah is still playing hard ball.

"Well, we will find out something else that works. We will strive hard till we meet your goals, but we need assurance from you that you will work with us for at least the next five years."

"Son, I am running a business here. I know I have taken care of people around me but they are dedicated to me for my whole life. I have not spent on them, I have invested in them. But the situation between you and me is different. You are a company and you have to prove yourself. I can't treat you the way I treat my employees."

"Fair enough. I understand what you are saying. If our campaign is not successful, then you won't work with us. This is quite clear to me. But what if it works? What if we are able to sell your one-ton murukku and create a demand in young customers?"

"Then, I will sign a five year contract with your company. You have my word."

"Thank you, sir. This helps a lot. But I have a request. Can we sign this as a contract now?"

"Why? Don't you believe my word?"

"I completely believe you, Mr Ramaiah. But as I said, my company is in a dire state. Investors are after me, although I am not the one who has created this situation. I need something to take back. I need something to show them. I need something to calm their nerves."

"Ok. Fair enough. I will sign and send the document to your office this evening. If you find a way to crack the market and sell one-ton murukku in an evening to young customers, then you get a five year contract. Otherwise, pay for the murukku and the ad campaign and not approach us for three years."

"Sir, I have one last request."

"Yes?"

"If we are successful in this campaign, then I want you to waive off the charges for murukku and the ad campaign." Sid was pushing his luck to the extreme.

Ramaiah pauses to think.

"No. That won't work. The best I can do is, I can waive off the amount for murukku and pay off the charges for the ad campaign but recover from your fees for the next five years."

"Done. That would be very helpful."

Ramaiah was like a coconut, hard from the outside but soft

at heart. He likes Sid's confidence and is willing to help him save his company.

Sid gets up, folds his hand and takes leave. On his way back, he again sees the poster that says, *What got you here, will not take you further*. Sid has forgotten everything that got him there and is only focused on what would bring him closer to his goal of saving his company.

When he reaches back to his office, Jo and Jee are still busy crunching numbers. From their faces, Sid can make out that they have cracked the problem.

Jee excitedly says, "The sampling followed by sales worked like magic. Most pubs accepted our offer. Now, I think we have sufficient pubs to try our virtual market place."

Jo says, "I checked the prices, the margins and the number of snacks consumed by each patron. With the number of pubs Jee has signed, I think we will be able push the required quantity out. In fact, I have a little extra margin in case we are required to drop the price or pay some additional incentive to the pub owners."

Jee says, "Sid, I think we are all set."

Sid says, "No, guys. I am still not convinced. You took care of the product, the price, and the place but what about the emotional connection. Why would the people suddenly start buying this unknown 'Fun Fries' just because we have kept them there? How will we win them over?"

Jo says, "We have to take our chances, Sid."

Sid says, "This is the last chance we have. There are no more chances after this. Ramaiah clearly mentioned that if we fail this time, he will not work with us for the next three years."

Jee says, "In that case, we are screwed, dude. We have no other clients left. In the next few months, all the termination notices will be served, and we will not have any client."

Jo says, "Don't be so negative. We will do something."

Sid says, "Yes. We have to stay positive for sure."

Jee says, "If we had even a little bit of leeway to spend on media, I am sure I would have come up with something that is catchy and makes our target customers aware of the product."

Sid says, "Don't even dream of spending money. Whatever little we have, I want to keep it to pay salaries for the next few months, just in case things go south."

Jee says, "We have no money and we need an ad campaign that will help us connect with the younger audience, correct?"

Sid says, "Yes, that is correct."

Sid, Jee and Jo take a break to think about this.

CHAPTER 20

Presence of Mind—
The Greatest Weapon

The best solutions lie beyond conventional boundaries.

Birbal and the Greatest Weapon

O*ne day, Akbar asks a question in the court. "What do you think is the best weapon in the world?"*

Some say, "Sword, of course. It is sharp, strong, and reliable."

Some say, "Bow and arrow. It can launch surprise attacks. You can kill the enemy from a distance."

Some say, "Spear, because it has virtues of both sword and bow and arrow."

Some say something else.

Akbar notices that Birbal is quiet. He repeats his question to Birbal, "Birbal, what do you think?"

Birbal says, "Jahanpanah, presence of mind is the best weapon. If you have a presence of mind, you can win with any weapon or even if you don't have one."

Everyone in the court laughs. Akbar is intrigued.

A few days later, a musth elephant is on the loose on the main streets of the city. The male elephant is running havoc and stamping the shops and people around them. Some warriors are running behind the elephant with swords, bow and arrow, spears and other weapons. But they can't control the elephant. Birbal is also walking along the same street, lost in his thoughts.

When he notices the musth elephant, he has no time to run or hide. He looks around and there is a stray dog walking by. He picks up the stray dog, holds it by hind legs and throws it toward the elephant's head. A barking dog hits the elephants head with great force. This surprises the elephant and he calms down. The mahoot rushes there to control the elephant. The dog is hurt but safe.

Birbal smiles at Akbar and says, "What presence of mind could do, other weapons could not." Akbar agrees.

Jo says, "How can we create something that reaches our target audience without spending any money?"

Sid looks up from his book. "We need a presence of mind. That is going to be our best weapon."

As Sid is saying this, Jee's phone beeps several times. He checks the phone and sees that he has received a few too many forwards from his group of friends. He is very irritated. He curses and says, "I am sick of these forwards. I hate them but everyone seems to love them."

Jo and Sid look at each other and shout, "Eureka!"

Jo jumps across the table, blowing kisses and gives a tight hug to Jee. Jee struggles to shake her off. Sid almost jumps on him, too.

"What did I do now?"

"You solved the problem! All youngsters love forwards, that's what you said, right? That is how our campaign will spread. We have to create messages that youngsters would love to forward!"

Jee says, "Oh yeah! Why didn't I think of that."

224

"You did. You just didn't know you did!"

They all laugh.

Jee says, "I have one more idea on how we can do the forwards."

Sid says, "Tell us."

Jee says, "I have noticed something new in the forwards I get. It is a TikTok video."

He pulls out one of the forwards and shows it to them. Sid and Jo have never seen it before. It is a 20-second video clip, which has a pre-recorded background track and anyone can use their phone and lip-sync and act on the track. They observed some of the videos; they range from hilarious to mildly annoying. Once the videos are recorded, you can forward them to your friends and they can go viral depending on the content. Jee shows that he received the same TikTok video in multiple groups.

Sid says, "This is brilliant. I think we have found our silver bullet. Let us create campaigns around JPEG forwards and TikTok videos."

Both Jo and Jee are excited. They have been working nonstop since the early morning. It is well past dinner time, but they don't care. They feel energized and want to create the campaign the same day.

Sid sits back and smiles to himself. This is his legacy, this is where he belongs, this is what he has created from scratch.

It is going to be a long night. Jo and Jee are animatedly discussing their ideas. He picks up the phone and orders food for all three of them.

He checks his mail. Paul has sent him the signed agreement. He has also received the agreement from Ramaiah about a potential five-year contract with stringent conditions. He signs both agreements and puts them in the out tray to be mailed back the next day.

It has been a long day. Fortunes have swung in his favor in just one day. In the morning, he was a minority stakeholder in the company, which had only one client who wasn't fully committed to them. By evening, he has signed two agreements, one that makes him a majority shareholder and another that gives him a steady revenue line for the next five years.

But everything hinges on how the virtual market for Fun Fries will work out two weeks later.

The day of the virtual marketplace campaign dawns. Jo, Jee, and Sid all are nervous. They have worked nonstop for two weeks. They have spent most of their time in Sid's office. They went home only to take a shower and change clothes once every two to three days. The campaign went through numerous iterations. It saw a lot of heated discussions, debates, and table-thumping to bring out the best.

But the final campaign is something all three of them are proud of. Their campaign relies very heavily on the target customers liking the campaign, and most importantly, feeling like it's worth forwarding to their friends. Jee had estimated that it took about a week for the TikTok video track to go viral. A few tiktokers chance upon it, like the track, record their own version, and forward it to their friends. If their friends like it, they will search for the same track on the TikTok app, record their own video, and circulate it to their friends.

If sufficient youngsters like it, the video goes viral and the viewership goes to millions in a short span. Jo has created some punchy soundtracks that position Fun Fries as the cool new snack, better than French fries or peanuts which are the most popular evening snacks. Jee and Jo recorded their first video, sent it to their friends, and waited patiently for viewership to go up. They also created some cool pictures that can be forwarded on WhatsApp and sent to their friend circle.

Sid, meanwhile, has worked with LTR to get the packs organized and send them to pubs. He has distributed samples to pub owners to win them over. To his surprise, none of them could guess that they were from LTR because of the shape and packing. The logistics piece was done and by today evening, curtains were going up for the virtual marketplace. By that night, the fate of everyone associated with Creativity Unlimited would be sealed.

Jee has gotten the entire office to work on this project. Everyone knows it's a do-or-die situation. Jee has allocated three pubs to each of the buddies. They are supposed to monitor each pub to check if the pub owner is distributing the samples correctly. They need to ensure the product is displayed prominently at all times.

They are also expected to talk to some customers informally and check their feedback about the product. In the end, they are supposed to report the quantity consumed in each pub on an hourly basis to Jee.

Jo and Jee have converted Sid's office into a war room. They have printed out the names of every pub and its broad profile and stuck it on a whiteboard. Under that, they have provided space for writing the quantity consumed every hour, feedback, and a few other details. Jo has created an Excel sheet to compile the numbers and come up with quantity projections for the day. Sid has to quickly analyze the data and take corrective action as quickly as possible.

The whole Creativity Unlimited is ready for the action. The next few hours are going to decide whether their beloved company survives or not. It hasn't been an easy journey for any of them. It has been long hard work, sleepless nights, rising to occasions, and going above and beyond themselves. Fortunately, they have enjoyed all of that. It's unfortunate that they have to be in this situation, the result of someone's selfish decisions for commercial gain.

But under Sid's leadership, they are all ready to fight. They all are determined to turn the tide. They all have one goal—to make their Fun Fries talk of the town for the next few hours. If that happens, they will get back their company, their freedom, their life, and their mojo which has been missing off-late.

It is about 7 PM when all buddies have taken their positions. They have talked to all pub owners, the waiters. They have kept them in good humor, told them what they needed and how they could do it without disturbing their patrons. Jee has spoken to all of them. Their group chats are buzzing with positivity.

As a group, they have faced many challenges and overcome them. They are quite sure this challenge, although the most daunting, won't be an exception. All of them are waiting for patrons to arrive and for the action to start.

The game plan is each group of customers would be served a free bowl full of Fun Fries with their first order. Once they finish their free bowl, the waiter is supposed to ask them for their opinion and if they would like to order more. If they say yes, they will have to pay for it. The waiter will ask them for refills with every order. The company is confident most of the patrons will say yes and the Fun Fries will fly off the shelf.

Patrons start trickling in at about 7–7:30 p.m. The vantage spots start to fill up. First orders are placed, and the first batch of Fun Fries is served. Drinks have started to flow and youth are warming up for a long evening. The buddies who are supposed to observe the pubs keep watching the tubs of the Fun Fries. They feel encouraged to see that most customers are reaching out to the tub.

They appreciate the snack. Some are peering at it closely, and some look like they are chatting about it. The first batch is gone in no time. Now the whole company is holding their breath to see if people will reorder it—that is the true test.

As planned, the waiters casually ask about reorders. Some of the customers agree, but most of them don't. The observant buddies take note of how many packs of Fun Fries are sold and move over to the next pub. They need to cover all the assigned pubs within every hour. Every pub they go to seems to be facing the same situation. They make their notes and report to Jee in their group chat.

Jee, in turn, goes to the war room whiteboard and updates the numbers. Jo quickly compiles all the numbers in her spreadsheet and soon all three of them are looking at early results. They are in for a shock because they are clearly way off the mark. They have about five hours to sell their one ton of Fun Fries. Logically, this means they should sell an average of 200 kilograms per hour. But Jo has studied the footfall pattern, and she has concluded that the sales will not be uniform every hour.

It will probably start slowly, peak around 10 p.m., and gradually reduce again. So she has projected that they would sell about 100 kilograms from 7 to 8 p.m., then 150 kilograms from 8 to 9 p.m., go to 250 kilograms from 9 to 10 p.m., and then peak at 10 to 11 p.m. with 400 kilograms. Then, it would drop back again to 100 kilograms from 11 to midnight.

To their dismay, sales are abysmal at the end of the first hour. Instead of 100 kilograms, they have sold only 20 kilograms. The three of them exchange worried glances. Sid tries to rally the troops. "Let's stay positive, guys. It's early in the evening, I am sure things will pick up soon."

Jee says, "Yes, I think so, too. It is like a one-day cricket match. Just because the first three overs are low scoring doesn't mean we will not reach the required score."

Jo frowns skeptically. She says, "Guys, these arguments have no meaning. Virat Kohli scoring runs has nothing to do with selling our Fun Fries. Don't be ridiculous. We need to do something here."

Jee says, "What?"

Jo says, "That's what we need to think, dumbo."

Sid gets what Jo is trying to say.

"Can you double-check the price again? Are you sure we have priced it correctly?"

Jo pulls out her Excel sheet and checks all the calculations again. There is nothing amiss.

"Yes, Sid. The Fun Fries are still accurately priced as compared to the other snack options."

Jee says, "Let us ask our teams to check if the pub owners have changed any prices today or if there are any other promotions going on."

"Yes, good idea," says Sid.

Jee immediately gets on his group chats and tells his field team to check and report the prices of other snacks. In 10–15 minutes, the patrons start trickling in. Jo enters them in the spreadsheet to check if anything has changed. Nothing has changed. The buddies in the field team don't have the complete picture as they are just focused on their own assigned pubs. In the next hour, they report increased sales.

Jee and Jo compile the numbers. It has certainly increased. From 20 kilograms in the first hour, it has jumped to 80 kilograms. But it is still miles away from what they need. Plus, low sales in the first two hours have created a void that needs to be filled in the next three hours.

The air of positivity has quickly dissolved into worried determination. But . . . what can they do? This is truly the worst pitfall of being the first to do something—they don't have a reference to know what their next step should be.

That is when Sid's phone rings. It's Ramaiah. Sid steps out of the room to take the call. When he comes back inside, he looks a little more desperate.

"Guys, we need to do something. I don't think we will reach our goal if we allow this to continue."

"But what? The only thing I can think of doing is running over to those pubs and buying all the Fun Fries myself. If only I had the cash to spare," Jee says miserably.

Jo spins around to look at him. Jee takes a wary step back at the crazed look of shock and joy on her face.

"YOU JEENIUS. You hit the nail on the head again! I think I have a plan, guys. All three of us need to be actual soldiers in this war instead of hunkering down in this war room. We have to go to pubs where we can see some known faces and go and buy them one more round of Fun Fries."

Jee says, "Okay, but how will that make a difference?"

"We're going to do more than just buy the snacks. We're going to be brand advocates! Nudge them to buy more Fun Fries, mingle, and have some fun. I think if we head down there, we can be a part of the solution in turning this around."

Sid can see where this is going and is already excited. He nods, "Yes, I agree! All three of us away from the action is not such a good idea. We have already wasted two hours. Let's go, guys!"

Jo says, "It will take some time for us to reach, so let's mobilize the field teams to start doing this too."

Suddenly, the war room is vacated. They have told their field team to abandon the monitoring activity and join their friends or acquaintances for a drink. Buy them a few tubs of Fun Fries, spend some time at the table, and move to the next table and do the same. Some of their teammates are tired of running around and welcome this idea. They join their friends, and order a few drinks and a few tubs of Fun Fries.

Most tables reordered the Fun Fries as they liked the taste. This continues for the next thirty minutes or so until Jo, Jee, and Sid arrive at the scene. By then, the sales of Fun Fries reached a respectable level of 100 kilograms in that hour. However, the next three hours are crucial. The trio is well aware of that. It is their presence of mind, analysis, and actions that are going to determine whether their company survives or not.

As soon as they reach, Jee is welcomed by a large group of long-time pals. He joins them with some hugs and hi-fives and starts chatting. He orders three tubs of Fun Fries to the table and many of them reach for it without thinking, with quite a few appreciating the taste between munches.

Sid is a well-known face because of the publicity he got in the business magazines. As soon as he reaches the pub, someone calls out to him and invites him to join their group. He gets a whiskey thrust into his hand and is asked if he has a snack preference. Pretending to think, he asks the waiter for something new and interesting. The waiter recommends the Fun Fries. He orders a few tubs, and the group continues chatting.

Jo, however, takes a step back from this plan. She isn't in the mood to mingle or drink and knows this won't help them sell 830 kilograms of the Fun Fries in the next three hours. She knows something is missing and looks around for ideas; it's right there in her mind, but she isn't quite able to put a finger on it. So she sits at a bar table, and pulls out her laptop so that she can pretend she is working while observing the entire pub.

She is sitting in the Pump House. It's a dimly lit, noisy pub. All the guests, young and old, are drinking and enjoying themselves. The drinks are flowing freely and so is their laughter. When a popular music number is played, guests from most tables try to sing along and create another wave of laughter.

After a while, she notices that in each group there are a few members who are not as talkative or they may not sing but they are looking at their phones. They are still part of the group but they are spending more time on their screens than talking to people. She also observes that they are continuously responding to their social media. If they receive something interesting, they show it to others and quickly forward it to everyone at the table.

Soon all of them take their phones out, check out the forward, respond to it, and perhaps send it to other groups before keeping the phones back. So most of the groups are interacting with friends around them as well as friends in cyberspace. It is a unique concoction of the real and virtual world. Pondering over this atypical way of interaction gives Jo the 'Aha!' moment she is looking for.

She realizes that they are only trying to reach customers in the physical space with their Fun Fries. But what about those in cyberspace? They have assumed that their campaign of TikTok videos and forwards is well received by their audience and they would act based on what they have seen. But that assumption may not be a very good one.

She thinks to herself, *They must be receiving hundreds of updates every day. How are we sure that everyone sitting in the pub has seen that campaign? And even if they have, how can they assume that they will recall the product Fun Fries at that moment and act based on that? This needs to be fixed.*

She steps out of the pub and calls Sid and Jee on a conference call. It takes a while for both to step out and take her call. Jo is growing impatient. As soon as they are connected, she almost starts yelling, "Guys! We're missing a MAJOR trick in a digital campaign! We haven't even tried to push this in cyberspace! These people in the pubs may not even have seen the campaign and may not even remember what they have seen!"

Sid says, "Oh shoot, you might be right!"

Jee says, "I don't get it. I checked the TikTok video profile, it has already crossed one lakh views, which is quite healthy. I have received some forwards myself, which indicates that these forwards are in circulation."

Jo snaps back, "Dude, I don't care if the total views are one lakh or one crore. I am here in one of the best pubs we have targeted, and nobody has made any reference to our TikTok or product, there's zero buzz around the Fun Fries."

Sid says, "You are right. I have seen some groups ordering the tubs, but the buzz is definitely missing. This is the biggest advantage of leaving our war room in the office and coming to ground zero."

Jo says, "You hit the nail on the head, Sid. That's why we are here."

Jee is still reticent as always. He says, "But what can we do? We can't send our TikToks and forwards to everyone sitting in the pub."

Jo takes a minute and says, "I KNOW! We switch on our Bluetooth and airdrop connections and push the video into as many phones as we can. We may not be able to reach everyone, but even if we reach one per table that is enough."

After that, she narrates her observation of how a few guests at each table are always looking at their phones and how they are pushing the content to those who are not looking at their phones.

"This is worth a try but I am not sure about the success rate," Jee says.

Sid says, "We don't know what is going to work so if it's worth a try we should go for it."

"Okay. Three of us should do it first and then tell all our buddies to do it, too. I will call you in ten minutes and update you. Bye."

CHAPTER 21

The Final Push

Putting your best foot forward sets the path to victory.

Jo rushes back to her refuge at the corner bar table. She orders one more orange juice to keep the bartender busy. She then switches on her Bluetooth. She is amazed to see that a large number of guests are available on Bluetooth and she can easily airdrop the videos to them. She is not sure if they will like it, but she decides to try it anyway. They, as a team, are with their back to the wall, so she's ready to try anything that could work.

She airdrops her first TikTok video to ten names she can see on her screen. Seven out of them accept the video and start playing it. It is a funny 15-second video, she can see some customers looking at it and laughing. They start showing it to their friends on the table and they all have a hearty laugh. Soon, they order the Fun Fries on their own. Making sure that communication reaches the customer at the point of consumption has always worked wonders. Jo is glad she was able to do it.

She then realizes that she is sitting in a corner of the pub. So she will have only a small fraction of guests in her Bluetooth range. She moves to the center of the pub and she sees more new names appearing on the screen. She pushes the video to all of them. Some of them accept, some don't. But at least things are moving.

She then strolls outside the pub where some guests are waiting to enter. Their names also appear on the screen, she pushes the video to them. Again the response is quite mixed. As she goes back to her spot, she is heartened to see more waiters bringing out tubs of Fun Fries. Could she have solved their problem?

She steps out again and calls both Sid and Jee. She explains what she has done and how she thinks that things would have started moving. Sid and Jee have also tried a similar approach. Although they haven't observed an increase in uptake of the Fun Fries, they have seen a fair number of guests accepting the videos.

Jo says, "I think this is going to work."

Jee says, "Yes. It's definitely worth a try."

Sid says, "Okay. Let us do it, guys. As we all know, 'Something is better than . . .'"

"Nothing," Both Jee and Jo say in a chorus.

Jee immediately puts a detailed list of what and how on the group chat. He also calls some buddies who are at various pubs to ensure they get going, and that they understand what to do. He asks them to report the results on a group chat every fifteen minutes. Jo goes back to her place, opens her laptop, and starts monitoring the views on the TikTok videos. They are growing at a steady pace. That is the indicator she is going to watch for the next few hours.

Sid goes back to his table and continues with his discussions. He doesn't have to push any forwards or videos. His buddies are sure to take care of that activity. He finishes his drink and moves to the next pub. All he has to do is to keep his army of buddies motivated. He reaches the pub and looks out for the buddy who is deployed there.

"Hey! How are you doing, Zee?"

"Sid, I am doing good. How are you?"

"I am good, too. Did Jee talk to you?"

"Yes. He did. I am pushing the videos, boss!"

"Great, Zee. I knew you all would. You all are amazing. Oh, but wait, have you had dinner yet?"

"Err hmm. I don't remember. I guess not."

"Ok, I think you need to eat first. We have a long night," Sid says.

"No, Sid, I am fine. We need to push this," Zee tries to evade.

"I insist," Sid says.

Sid orders a club sandwich and ensures Zee eats it. Even Zee doesn't realize that he was so hungry. He gobbles up the sandwich and reaches for his wallet. Sid stops him and says, "This is on me. You carry on."

Zee pulls out his phone again and rushes back to the pub to see if there are any new patrons where he can push the videos and forwards.

Sid knows what he has to do. He moves to the next pub, meets another hardworking, reluctant-to-eat buddy and orders another club sandwich.

In the meanwhile, Jee rushes to the pub where Jo is sitting. They always produce the best results when they are together. They start to monitor the viewership of various TikTok videos which are steadily growing. Jee thinks of another idea—he puts all the forwards on his Facebook, Pinterest, Snapchat, etc. They are doing all-out efforts in cyberspace to reach out to their customers.

Things start to move. In the next hour, they surpass the target they had kept for themselves. They clock a whopping 250 kilograms in that one hour. They see the light at the end of the tunnel, but still feel like they are not there yet. The rate needs to pick up more. They can't take any chances.

Jo starts her investigation again. She says, "Jee, how many videos are in circulation now?"

Jee says, "Five. We had recorded them in the beginning."

Jo says, "Is that enough?"

"Under normal circumstances more than enough."

Jo quips, "But these are not normal circumstances, right? We need more."

Jee says, "Listen, what is happening the best under the circumstances. If we want to step up the circulation, we need more videos. Videos showing different people have different forward rates. If there is something appealing, something different, something local, the forwards are more."

Jo says, "Okay, so let us make that happen."

Jee says, "How?"

Jo gets up. Grabs Jee by arm and walks to the middle of the pub. She then opens the TikTok Video app and starts recording. They know the soundtrack by heart. So both of them act and lip sync on the video and in the end, show the real Fun Fries pack in the video. They do a couple of takes to perfect the video. Then, they take a final look at it, laugh it out and share it on their social media network.

BULLSEYE. The response to their video is instantaneous. Their friends not only like their videos, but are also actively forward them. They get it back from different groups. They can see that things have started moving.

Jee starts monitoring the TikTok video views, which are now growing at an even faster pace than before. Jo goes back to her observation of the pub patrons. She still looks worried. Irrespective of the internet statistics, she still thinks the on-ground buzz is missing. She thinks that their video is received by a few patrons sitting in the pub, who recognize that it was shot very close to them. They watch it, share it and laugh.

All of a sudden, another couple in the same pub, walks to the center, opens their TikTok app and records their video. They then get back to their table and forward it and post it on Facebook and Instagram. After a few moments of silence, some phones on other tables start beeping. The freshly recorded video has traveled through cyberspace to reach tables next to them. That motivates a few on tables to record their TikTok video about Fun Fries.

Soon, the snowballing effect of digital media takes over. Hundreds of youth across all the pubs start recording their own version of TikTok videos about Fun Fries and circulating it. The buzz that was missing is now almost tangible. Customers are not just interacting with the brand, but are also recommending it by forwarding it to their friends. Needless to say, the orders for Fun Fries are shooting up. After the brand is seen in the video, they see it in the store and then they see the promotion and naturally, they place the order.

They have managed to get the ball rolling. Now, they want to see how far it moves.

Jo tries to call buddies located in other pubs but it's too noisy. She can't hear a thing. Since she has asked them to spend time with their friends, she can't expect them to chat. She starts to feel impatient. She taps on Jee's shoulders and signals, "It's time to go back to the war room."

They don't have time to get back to the office. They go to a nearby coffee shop that offers them ample space and a quiet atmosphere to work. They ask Sid to join them.

Jee gets on with his number counting again. It's fifteen minutes past eleven and they are eagerly awaiting the numbers to add up. Their efforts in the past hour or so have paid handsome dividends.

They have sold 400 kilograms of murukku in the last one hour. There are smiles everywhere. All three of them give each other a small hi-five.

But they do realize that the job is far from over. They still have to sell about 230 kilograms and just about forty-five minutes to one hour is left. It is not an easy task. Moreover, they have played all their cards now and it's left to their combined fates.

When you are striving to achieve a lofty goal, you invariably reach this situation. You have done all you can, but there are still some unknown, uncertain factors involved. Some call it God, some call it fate, and some call it probabilities. But it all means the same thing. It means you have to wait.

You have to wait patiently for the result to unfold. You have to feel proud of all the efforts you put in, you have to own up to all the decisions you had to make all along, you have to own up the flaws; you have to focus on the right things you did and you have to stay optimistic about the outcome. But at the same time, you must be equally open to things not going as per your expectations. You have to be open to you missing the goal by a whisker, you have to be open for any outcome.

As you are waiting, you can pray to your favourite God or you can try to distract your mind or you can call your mom or you can go to sleep. No matter what you do, the outcome doesn't change. But what you do merely prepares yourself for accepting the outcome.

Jo prays to the Lord Ganesha. Jee distracts himself by playing a video game. Sid calls his mother. He says to himself, once all this is over he will call Anjali. The remaining hour passes in a jiffy.

With throbbing hearts and nervous minds, they start collecting the numbers. Jo and Jee are calling everyone and collecting the numbers for the last hour but also checking if numbers collected throughout the evening are accurate. Sid is calling each buddy and thanking him or her for efforts and support. He is truly grateful to all of them for the relentless efforts to achieve their common goal.

He thinks to himself, *As long as I have such a team behind me, I can do anything. I can achieve any goal no matter how difficult it is.*

Jo and Jee have collected the numbers, cross-checked and entered their excel sheet. Now someone has to press a button so that the total is displayed on the screen. Nobody dares. This click is going to decide the fate of unrelenting efforts, tears and sweat shed by all the buddies, heartburn faced by Sid and the future of the Creativity Unlimited. This is the final moment—the moment of truth.

They ask Sid to press the button. As Sid is about to press the button, Jo stops him and says her final prayer to the Lord Ganesha. Jee can't take the excitement, he is looking out of the window. Sid is nervous too.

The number is displayed on the screen. They can't believe their eyes. This was the number which they hoped would rewrite their fortune but it wasn't to be. The number displayed on the screen was just 900. They had failed to achieve the glorious figure of 1,000. They made all-out efforts, they fought well, they came tantalizingly close but they failed.

Jo starts crying; Jee thumps his fist on the table and gets up and leaves the room. Sid is dumbstruck, doesn't know how to react. For the past few months, he had put in all his energy and hopes so that he would not be in this situation. But he hadn't thought about what he would do if it came to be.

Moments of silence pass. Jee enters the room. Jo wipes her tears. Sid has absorbed the shock.

"Now what?" Jee asks.

Jo looks away.

Sid clears his throat and says, "First and foremost, I must visit Ramaiah in the morning and update him on the results."

"Do you think he will give us one more chance? Do you think he will consider this a success?" Jee asks.

Sid says, "No way. He is a straightforward person. He will go by the books. Now we have legal agreements in place. So there is no chance that he will deviate. We have to face the inevitable."

"What about the company? What about other clients? What about all the money you have to pay back?"

"I don't know, guys. I never got a chance to think about that. I will take it one step at a time."

"Hmm."

"Right now, I neither have the answers to all questions nor do I know where to find them."

"Right."

"We have been working nonstop for days together. We need some rest. I am sure we will find some way."

Jo quips, "I am not sure about that, but yes, we need some rest."

Sid says, "Let me call Ola-taxi for you guys."

"What about you?" Jo asks.

"I will sleep here. I don't know how many chances I will get to stay in this office. Let me seize whatever I can get."

"Then we're staying too," says Jo

Jee says, "Yes, that's right, we want to stay here, too. This room is as much ours as it is yours."

They all give each other a group hug.

They pull out three separate beds, crank up the air conditioner and lie down, trying to go to sleep.

CHAPTER 22

Expect the Unexpected

Give your best and let luck handle the rest.

The next day, Sid is supposed to see Ramaiah at 9 a.m. Jo and Jee insist on coming along. They have kept special attire in their drawers to wear for LTR meetings. Soon, they are seated in Ramaiah's cabin. They are served the filter coffee and they are waiting for Ramaiah to arrive.

Jee whispers in Jo's ears, "Dude, this may be the last time we may be seeing Ram-dude and his cabin and drinking his filter coffee."

Jo says, "Yeah, I was thinking the same. It is kinda weird, right."

Jee is about to say something when Ramaiah enters the cabin.

All three of them get up with folded hands. Ramaiah does likewise.

"How are you, Siddharth, Jyotichandrika, and Jeetendraprasad?"

All three of them are used to being addressed by their birth names.

"We are good," says Sid.

"So, how was your promotion yesterday evening? Did we achieve the goal?"

From the tone of the question, Sid senses that Ramaiah knows what has happened. He is purposely blank faced. Maybe he was tracking the sales independently or he was not optimistic about the results or perhaps he had a sixth sense.

"We tried our best. We gave it our best shot. We came up with several innovative ideas," says Sid.

"Okay. Interesting. Did we achieve our target?" Ramaiah is to the point, as always.

"No, sir. We fell short. We came very close. But we could not sell all of it."

"Hmm."

"I wouldn't see this as a failure because if you look at our overall goal of increasing acceptance of your products among young customers, that happened, but we could not surpass the pre-agreed number."

"Right. I understand."

"We are aware of what that means. It means that you will neither offer us a further contract nor can we contact you for three more years. Also, we now have to pay the price of murukku and the advertisement campaign we ran previously."

"I am glad you understand."

"This is a huge challenge for us. We don't have enough money or resources to honor our commitments but that is completely our problem. We need to do what we can to make the payments."

"Right," said Ramaiah. His expression is still curiously blank.

"We want to thank you from the bottom of our hearts for giving us this opportunity. It was great working with a thorough, professional client like you. Your team and the entire staff was very nice to us throughout the engagement. Thank you so much."

"Thank you, too," said Ramaiah

Sid looks at Jo and Jee from the corner of his eyes to check if he missed something. Both of them nod, and all three get up with folded hands.

"Thank you very much, Mr Ramaiah. Wish you all the best."

Ramaiah doesn't get up. He looks at them steadily. All three of them look at his office for one last time and return to the door. The famous sign on the door *What got you here may not take you further* sounds even more profound now.

As they are about to leave the room, Ramaiah says, "Wait."

All three turn around in astonishment.

"Sit down," says Ramaiah authoritatively.

"You may not have sold 1,000 kilograms of murukku, but you didn't fail to generate the demand from young customers."

"Really? How do you know?"

"I don't know what you did, but since 9 p.m. last night, I started getting calls from our distributors from across India informing me about some Fun Fries being sold in Bangalore. Then I got my team to check what they were saying, and I found that they were talking about murukku that I supplied you. My team confirmed this. They also showed me a video where both of you promote the product.

"I didn't understand what it was, but it did say Fun Fries. Some distributors even told me we should package our murukku similar to Fun Fries and sell. They believe that there is a strong market for that. Just a few distributors who called me last night are ready to buy your Fun Chips. They are saying it will sell maybe ten times more than the murukku. That is sensational."

"What are you saying, Mr Ramaiah? That is so good and so hard to believe." Sid was too elated to find the correct expressions.

"I asked my men to buy some Fun Fries and try them out. Of course, it tastes like our murukku but looks different. It appeals to youngsters because of its unusual shape and is more nutritious than anything else."

"That is right."

"I think you have cracked the most difficult problem faced by my company. I knew you fell short of 100 kilograms. But I asked my men to buy back the 100 kilograms from those shops, so we don't have any legal hurdle to continue."

"That is unbelievable."

"So, congratulations, Mr Siddharth, Jyotichandrika, and Jeetendraprasad, for making it happen. I am glad to present to you our five-year contract for being our digital ad agency. We would be moving a substantial part of our TV and Newspaper budgets to digital media for youth and the conventional range. We hope your company benefits from this and does very well."

Mr Ramaiah extends his hand for a handshake. Sid has no words as he holds the hand with his hands, tears of joy streaming down his cheeks. Jo and Jee hug him from either side as they struggle to control their emotions. Suddenly, Sid's phone rings.

It's Anjali!

About the Author

Vivek Vaidya is a prominent figure in the Automotive Industry, recognized as a leading voice at international conferences and a sought-after analyst on global TV channels. As an Associate Partner at Frost & Sullivan, he guides global automotive companies in shaping their strategic growth and innovation plans. With a track record of delivering keynote speeches in cities like Tokyo, Seoul, Singapore, and London, Vivek has shared his insights on numerous platforms. His expertise has been showcased in over 300 TV interviews on channels such as BBC, CNBC, Bloomberg, Channel NewsAsia, and ET NOW.

Beyond his professional achievements, Vivek is a celebrated author renowned for his Marathi anthology collection *Aagantuk*, which earned him the prestigious Banahatti Award in Pune. His English short story collection, "Why Do Indians . . .?" has garnered widespread attention, with its second edition already circulating. Additionally, his poem "Anurup" was selected from a pool of entries to be featured on the prominent Marathi language YouTube channel, "Kaviteche Paan." Notably, Vivek has also made significant contributions to theater, with his multilingual plays "Matrudakshina" and "Subatomic Premier League" being showcased in prestigious playfests in Singapore.

Adding to his diverse repertoire, Vivek is an avid trekker, having conquered summits like Mt. Kilimanjaro, Everest Base Camp, Mt. Fuji, Tour Du Mont Blanc, Mt. Kinabalu, andMt. Rinjani. He leads the popular trekking enthusiast group trekkers@heart in Southeast Asia. Vivek is known for his versatility. He hosts stage shows and talk shows and explores interests in singing and stand-up comedy.

Educationally, Vivek holds a Master's in Management focusing on Marketing and a Bachelor of Engineering in Mechanical. Originally from Pune, he spent 13 years in Bengaluru before relocating to Singapore.